ENGLISH
FOR EVERYONE

PRACTICE BOOK

LEVEL ❷ BEGINNER

FREE AUDIO
website and app
www.dkefe.com

Author

Thomas Booth worked for 10 years as an English-language teacher in Poland and Russia. He now lives in England, where he works as an editor and English-language materials writer, notably of course books and vocabulary textbooks.

Course consultant

Tim Bowen has taught English and trained teachers in more than 30 countries worldwide. He is the co-author of works on pronunciation teaching and language-teaching methodology, and author of numerous books for English-language teachers. He is currently a freelance materials writer, editor, and translator. He is a member of the Chartered Institute of Linguists.

Language consultant

Professor Susan Barduhn is an experienced English-language teacher, teacher trainer, and author, who has contributed to numerous publications. In addition to directing English-language courses in at least four different continents, she has been President of the International Association of Teachers of English as a Foreign Language, and an adviser to the British Council and the US State Department. She is currently a Professor at the School for International Training in Vermont, USA.

ENGLISH
FOR EVERYONE

PRACTICE BOOK
LEVEL 2 BEGINNER

DK India
Senior Editors Vineetha Mokkil, Anita Kakar
Senior Art Editor Chhaya Sajwan
Project Editor Antara Moitra
Editors Agnibesh Das, Nisha Shaw, Seetha Natesh
Art Editors Namita, Heena Sharma, Sukriti Sobti,
Shipra Jain, Aanchal Singhal
Assistant Editors Ira Pundeer, Ateendriya Gupta,
Sneha Sunder Benjamin, Ankita Yadav
Assistant Art Editors Roshni Kapur,
Meenal Goel, Priyansha Tuli
Illustrators Ivy Roy, Arun Pottirayil, Bharti Karakoti, Rahul Kumar
Picture Researcher Deepak Negi
Managing Editor Pakshalika Jayaprakash
Managing Art Editor Arunesh Talapatra
Production Manager Pankaj Sharma
Pre-production Manager Balwant Singh
Senior DTP Designer Vishal Bhatia, Neeraj Bhatia
DTP Designer Sachin Gupta
Jacket Designer Surabhi Wadhwa
Managing Jackets Editor Saloni Singh
Senior DTP Designer (jackets) Harish Aggarwal

DK UK
Editorial Assistants Jessica Cawthra, Sarah Edwards
Illustrators Edwood Burn, Denise Joos, Michael Parkin,
Jemma Westing
Audio Producer Liz Hammond
Managing Editor Daniel Mills
Managing Art Editor Anna Hall
Project Manager Christine Stroyan
Jacket Designer Natalie Godwin
Jacket Editor Claire Gell
Jacket Design Development Manager Sophia MTT
Producer, Pre-Production Luca Frassinetti
Producer Mary Slater
Publisher Andrew Macintyre
Art Director Karen Self
Publishing Director Jonathan Metcalf

First published in Great Britain in 2016 by
Dorling Kindersley Limited
80 Strand, London, WC2R 0RL

A CIP catalogue record for this book
is available from the British Library.
ISBN: 978-0-2412-5270-3

Printed and bound in China

All images © Dorling Kindersley Limited
For further information see: www.dkimages.com

A WORLD OF IDEAS:
SEE ALL THERE IS TO KNOW

www.dk.com

Contents

How the course works

English for Everyone is designed for people who want to teach themselves the English language. Like all language courses, it covers the core skills: grammar, vocabulary, pronunciation, listening, speaking, reading, and writing. Unlike in other courses, the skills are taught and practiced as visually as possible, using images and graphics to help you understand and remember. The practice book is packed with exercises designed to reinforce the lessons you have learned in the course book. Work through the units in order, making full use of the audio available on the website and app.

COURSE BOOK

PRACTICE BOOK

Unit number The book is divided into units. Each practice book unit tests the language taught in the course book unit with the same number.

Practice points Every unit begins with a summary of the key practice points.

Modules Each unit is broken down into modules, which should be done in order. You can take a break from learning after completing any module.

Vocabulary Throughout the book, vocabulary pages test your memory of key English words and phrases taught in the course book.

Visual practice Images and graphics offer visual cues to help fix the most useful and important English words in your memory.

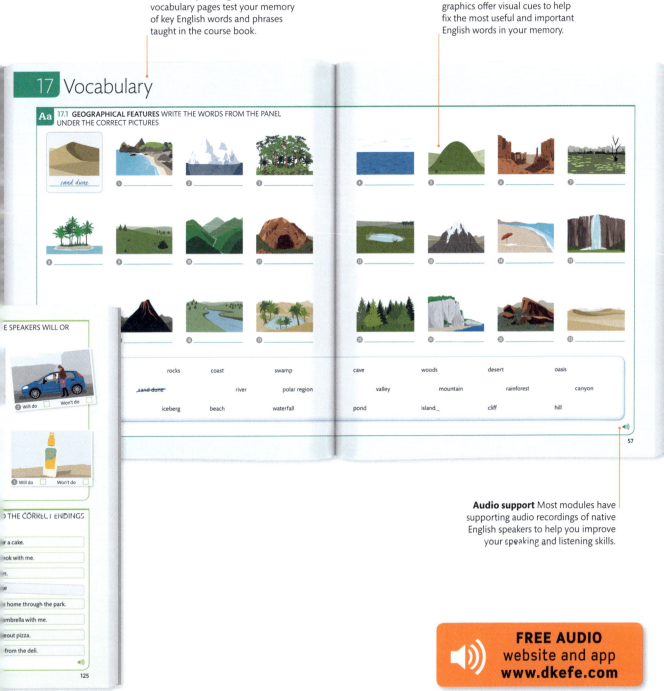

Audio support Most modules have supporting audio recordings of native English speakers to help you improve your speaking and listening skills.

FREE AUDIO
website and app
www.dkefe.com

Practice modules

Each exercise is carefully graded to drill and test the language taught in the corresponding course book units. Working through the exercises alongside the course book will help you remember what you have learned and become more fluent. Every exercise is introduced with a symbol to indicate which skill is being practiced.

GRAMMAR
Apply new language rules in different contexts.

READING
Examine target language in real-life English contexts.

LISTENING
Test your understanding of spoken English.

VOCABULARY
Cement your understanding of key vocabulary.

SPEAKING
Compare your spoken English to model audio recordings.

Module number Every module is identified with a unique number, so you can easily locate answers and related audio.

Exercise instruction Every exercise is introduced with a brief instruction, telling you what you need to do.

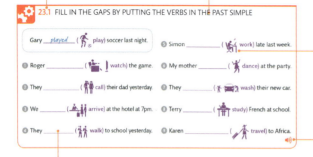

23.1 FILL IN THE GAPS BY PUTTING THE VERBS IN THE PAST SIMPLE

Gary _played_ (play) soccer last night.
① Roger _____ (watch) the game.
② They _____ (call) their dad yesterday.
③ We _____ (arrive) at the hotel at 7pm.
④ They _____ (walk) to school yesterday.
⑤ Simon _____ (work) late last week.
⑥ My mother _____ (dance) at the party.
⑦ They _____ (wash) their new car.
⑧ Terry _____ (study) French at school.
⑨ Karen _____ (travel) to Africa.

Supporting graphics Visual cues are given to help you understand the exercises.

Supporting audio This symbol shows that the answers to the exercise are available as audio tracks. Listen to them after completing the exercise.

Space for writing You are encouraged to write your answers in the book for future reference.

Sample answer The first question of each exercise is answered for you, to help make the task easy to understand.

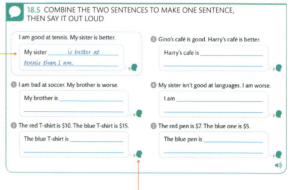

18.5 COMBINE THE TWO SENTENCES TO MAKE ONE SENTENCE, THEN SAY IT OUT LOUD

I am good at tennis. My sister is better.
My sister _is better at tennis than I am._
① I am bad at soccer. My brother is worse.
My brother is _____
② The red T-shirt is $10. The blue T-shirt is $15.
The blue T-shirt is _____
③ Gino's café is good. Harry's café is better.
Harry's cafe is _____
④ My sister isn't good at languages. I am worse.
I am _____
⑤ The red pen is $7. The blue one is $5.
The blue pen is _____

Listening exercise This symbol indicates that you should listen to an audio track in order to answer the questions in the exercise.

36.8 LISTEN TO THE AUDIO AND NUMBER THE PICTURES IN THE ORDER THEY ARE DESCRIBED

Speaking exercise This symbol indicates that you should say your answers out loud, then compare them to model recordings included in your audio files.

Audio

English for Everyone features extensive supporting audio materials. You are encouraged to use them as much as you can, to improve your understanding of spoken English, and to make your own accent and pronunciation more natural. Each file can be played, paused, and repeated as often as you like, until you are confident you understand what has been said.

LISTENING EXERCISES
This symbol indicates that you should listen to an audio track in order to answer the questions in the exercise.

SUPPORTING AUDIO
This symbol indicates that extra audio material is available for you to listen to after completing the module.

FREE AUDIO
website and app
www.dkefe.com

Answers

An answers section at the back of the book lists the correct answers for every exercise. Turn to these pages whenever you finish a module and compare your answers with the samples provided, to see how well you have understood each teaching point.

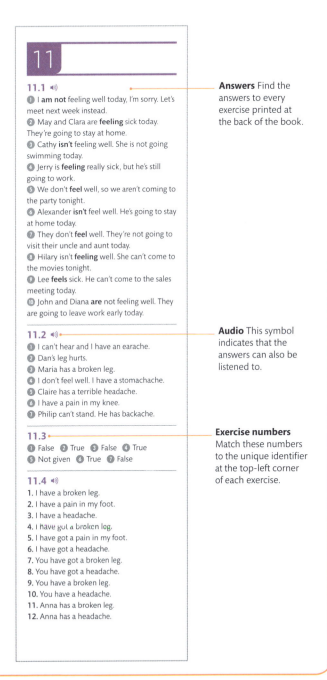

11.1
1. I **am not** feeling well today, I'm sorry. Let's meet next week instead.
2. May and Clara are **feeling** sick today. They're going to stay at home.
3. Cathy **isn't** feeling well. She is not going swimming today.
4. Jerry is **feeling** really sick, but he's still going to work.
5. We don't **feel** well, so we aren't coming to the party tonight.
6. Alexander **isn't** feel well. He's going to stay at home today.
7. They don't **feel** well. They're not going to visit their uncle and aunt today.
8. Hilary isn't **feeling** well. She can't come to the movies tonight.
9. Lee **feels** sick. He can't come to the sales meeting today.
10. John and Diana **are** not feeling well. They are going to leave work early today.

11.2
1. I can't hear and I have an earache.
2. Dan's leg hurts.
3. Maria has a broken leg.
4. I don't feel well. I have a stomachache.
5. Claire has a terrible headache.
6. I have a pain in my knee.
7. Philip can't stand. He has backache.

11.3
1. False 2. True 3. False 4. True
5. Not given 6. True 7. False

11.4
1. I have a broken leg.
2. I have a pain in my foot.
3. I have a headache.
4. I have got a broken leg.
5. I have got a pain in my foot.
6. I have got a headache.
7. You have got a broken leg.
8. You have got a headache.
9. You have a broken leg.
10. You have a headache.
11. Anna has a broken leg.
12. Anna has a headache.

Answers Find the answers to every exercise printed at the back of the book.

Audio This symbol indicates that the answers can also be listened to.

Exercise numbers Match these numbers to the unique identifier at the top-left corner of each exercise.

01 Talking about yourself

When you want to tell someone about yourself, or about people and things that relate to you, you use the present simple tense of "to be."

⚙ **New language** Using "to be"
Aa Vocabulary Names, jobs, and family
🧩 **New skill** Talking about yourself

1.1 CROSS OUT THE INCORRECT WORD IN EACH SENTENCE

Jack ~~are~~ / is 27 years old.

1 They **are** / **is** the Walker family.

2 You **am** / **are** a police officer.

3 Eve **is** / **are** from Canada.

4 I **is** / **am** a teacher.

5 We **are** / **is** Australian.

6 He **am** / **is** an artist.

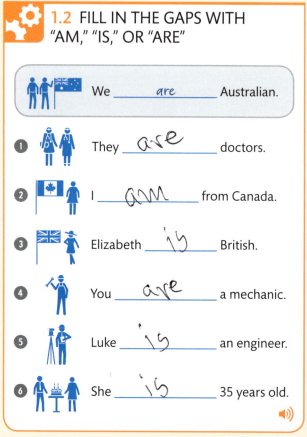

1.2 FILL IN THE GAPS WITH "AM," "IS," OR "ARE"

We _____are_____ Australian.

1 They ___are___ doctors.

2 I ___am___ from Canada.

3 Elizabeth ___is___ British.

4 You ___are___ a mechanic.

5 Luke ___is___ an engineer.

6 She ___is___ 35 years old.

1.3 USE THE CHART TO CREATE EIGHT CORRECT SENTENCES AND SAY THEM OUT LOUD

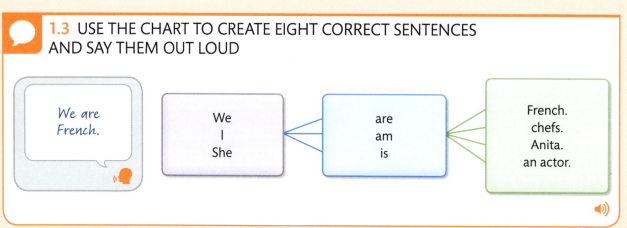

We are French.

| We / I / She | are / am / is | French. / chefs. / Anita. / an actor. |

1.4 FILL IN THE GAPS TO MAKE NEGATIVE SENTENCES

I _____am not_____ from Argentina.

1. John and Ellie _are not_ best friends.
2. Mr. Robbins _is not_ a teacher.
3. It _is not_ 2 o'clock.
4. You _are not_ my sister.
5. Annabelle _is not_ at school.
6. Ann and Ravi _are not_ students.
7. Ken _is not_ a mechanic.
8. We _are not_ doctors.
9. He _is not_ 45 years old.
10. They _are not_ my teachers.
11. She _is not_ from Ireland.
12. It _is not_ Martha's book.

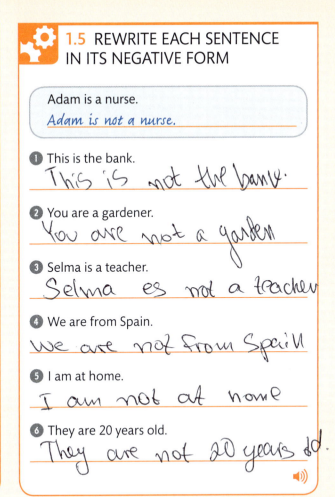

1.5 REWRITE EACH SENTENCE IN ITS NEGATIVE FORM

Adam is a nurse.
Adam is not a nurse.

1. This is the bank.
This is not the bank.

2. You are a gardener.
You are not a garden

3. Selma is a teacher.
Selma es not a teacher

4. We are from Spain.
We are not from Spain

5. I am at home.
I am not at home

6. They are 20 years old.
They are not 20 years old.

1.6 SAY THE QUESTIONS OUT LOUD, FILLING IN THE GAPS

_____Are_____ you from France?

1. _Are_ they your dogs?
2. _is_ Jo your cousin?
3. _is_ it 10 o'clock?
4. _am_ I in your class?
5. _Are_ you Canadian?
6. _Are_ those your keys?
7. _is_ Martin at work today?
8. _is_ Elena 28 years old?
9. _Are_ they nurses?

02 Talking about routines

You can use present simple statements to describe your daily routines, pastimes, and possessions. Use "do" to form negatives and ask questions.

⚙ **New language** The present simple
Aa Vocabulary Routines and pastimes
🧩 **New skill** Talking about routines

2.1 CROSS OUT THE INCORRECT WORD IN EACH SENTENCE

Eddie ~~live~~ / lives in Canada.

1 They ~~cook~~ / cooks pizza for dinner.

2 Your friend ~~has~~ / have a microwave.

3 She work / ~~works~~ at the gym.

4 I ~~watch~~ / watches TV every day.

5 We leaves / ~~leave~~ work at 5pm.

6 Mark ~~has~~ / have a skateboard.

7 They ~~start~~ / starts school at 9am.

8 You hates / ~~hate~~ soccer.

9 Tara eat / ~~eats~~ breakfast at 7:15am.

10 I ~~go~~ / goes to the park after work.

11 We wakes up / ~~wake up~~ at 7am.

12 He cook / ~~cooks~~ dinner at 8pm.

13 My son walks / ~~walk~~ to school.

🔊

2.2 FILL IN THE GAPS USING THE WORDS IN THE PANEL

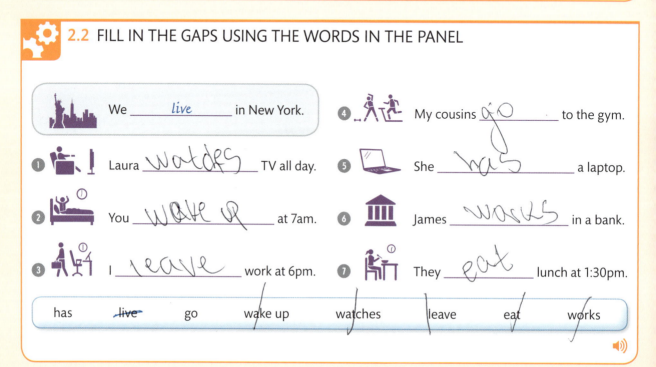

We ___live___ in New York.

1 Laura _watches_ TV all day.

2 You _wake up_ at 7am.

3 I _leave_ work at 6pm.

4 My cousins _go_ to the gym.

5 She _has_ a laptop.

6 James _works_ in a bank.

7 They _eat_ lunch at 1:30pm.

has   ~~live~~   go   wake up   watches   leave   eat   works

🔊

14

2.3 SAY THE SENTENCES OUT LOUD, FILLING IN THE GAPS

Omar __works__ (work) in an office.

7. They __start__ (start) work at 10am.

1. They __eat__ (eat) pizza for lunch.

8. Robert __has__ (have) a car.

2. Mia __get up__ (get up) late on Saturdays.

9. I __wake up__ (wake up) at 6:45am.

3. You __go__ (go) to work early.

10. Jay __studys__ (study) science every day.

4. We __cook__ (cook) dinner at 7:30pm.

11. Karen __likes__ (like) tennis.

5. Paul __finish__ (finish) work at 6pm.

12. He __works__ (work) in a school.

6. Lily __watches__ (watch) TV every day.

13. Jess __goes__ (go) to bed at 10pm.

2.4 LISTEN TO THE AUDIO, THEN NUMBER THE PICTURES IN THE ORDER THEY ARE DESCRIBED

A ☐

B 1

C ☐

D ☐

E ☐

F ☐

2.5 READ THE BLOG AND ANSWER THE QUESTIONS

Edward lives in Australia.
True ✓ **False** ☐ **Not given** ☐

❶ He gets up at 7:30am.
True ✓ **False** ☐ **Not given** ☐

❷ He doesn't work in an office.
True ✓ **False** ☐ **Not given** ☐

❸ He likes his job.
True ☐ **False** ☐ **Not given** ✓

❹ He has lunch with his friends.
True ✓ **False** ☐ **Not given** ☐

❺ He has a dog.
True ✓ **False** ☐ **Not given** ☐

❻ He goes swimming most weekends.
True ☐ **False** ✓ **Not given** ☐

MY DAY

HOME | ENTRIES | ABOUT | CONTACT

MY ROUTINE

Hi, my name's Edward. I live in Sydney, Australia. I get up at 7am every morning. I have breakfast at 7:30am and I take the bus to work. I start work at 9am every day. I don't work in an office. I'm a gardener and I work outside. I have lunch with my friends Steve and Vicky at 1pm. I leave work at 5:30pm. After work, I go swimming or I play tennis. In the evening I walk in the park with my dog. I go to bed at 10:30pm. Most weekends, I meet friends and I like watching movies. I like Sydney. It's a great city.

 2.6 MATCH THE BEGINNINGS OF THE SENTENCES TO THE CORRECT ENDINGS

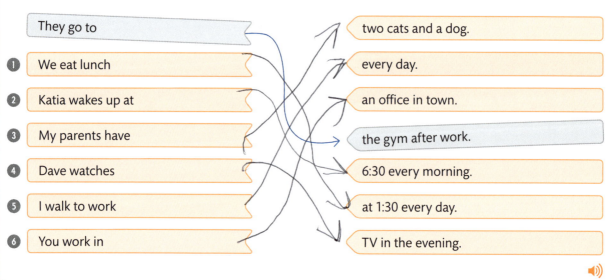

They go to

❶ We eat lunch

❷ Katia wakes up at

❸ My parents have

❹ Dave watches

❺ I walk to work

❻ You work in

two cats and a dog.

every day.

an office in town.

the gym after work.

6:30 every morning.

at 1:30 every day.

TV in the evening.

2.7 WRITE EACH SENTENCE TWO DIFFERENT WAYS

She lives in Britain.	She does not live in Britain.	She doesn't live in Britain.
1 I work in a school.		
2	Sam does not eat lunch at 1pm.	
3		We don't leave home at 7:45am.
4 They like pizza.		
5	Sia does not watch TV every day.	
6		My friend doesn't have a dog.
7 You get up early.		
8	I do not have a new coat.	
9		He doesn't finish work at 5:30pm.

2.8 USE THE CHARTS TO CREATE 15 CORRECT SENTENCES AND SAY THEM OUT LOUD

> *Lucy doesn't walk to work.*

Lucy I They	doesn't don't	walk get up eat	to work. early. breakfast.

> *Do you like cats?*

Do you Does John	like work	cats? soccer? in an office?

17

03 Today I'm wearing...

You can use the present continuous to describe something that is happening now. It is often used to describe what people are wearing, using, or doing.

 New language The present continuous
Aa Vocabulary Clothes and activities
New skill Talking about what's happening now

 3.1 CROSS OUT THE INCORRECT WORD IN EACH SENTENCE

> Sandra **is** / ~~are~~ having her dinner.

❶ Glen **is** / **are** cleaning his car.

❷ April **is** / **are** watching a film.

❸ Peter and Frank **is** / **are** wearing suits.

❹ James **is** / **are** painting the kitchen.

❺ We **is** / **are** traveling around China.

❻ You **is** / **are** listening to an interesting song.

❼ Doug **is** / **are** reading a newspaper.

3.2 LISTEN TO THE AUDIO, THEN NUMBER THE PICTURES IN THE ORDER THEY ARE DESCRIBED

Ⓐ ☐

Ⓑ ☐

Ⓒ 1

Ⓓ ☐

Ⓔ ☐

Ⓕ ☐

3.3 FILL IN THE GAPS BY PUTTING THE VERBS IN THE PRESENT CONTINUOUS

Mario _is walking_ (walk) his dog in the park.

1 Anne _____ (wait) for her brother.

2 Pedro _____ (cook) pizza for dinner.

3 Mike _____ (mow) the lawn.

4 Cynthia _____ (lie) on the sofa.

5 Jane _____ (go) to the theater.

6 I _____ (work) at the moment.

7 Colin _____ (listen) to some music.

8 Our children _____ (play) in a band.

9 We _____ (drink) lemonade.

10 Stefan _____ (come) to our party.

11 They _____ (eat) pasta for dinner.

12 Roberta _____ (wear) a sweater.

13 You _____ (play) tennis with John.

3.4 MATCH THE BEGINNINGS OF THE SENTENCES TO THE CORRECT ENDINGS

Julie doesn't usually wear dresses,

1 Paula doesn't often watch TV,

2 Sven usually cooks at home,

3 I often go to bed at 11pm,

4 Janet is working at home today,

5 Ravi usually wears casual clothes,

6 Tim usually has cereal for breakfast,

7 We usually go on vacation to Greece,

8 I almost always drive to work,

9 Nelson is drinking wine today,

10 You usually wear pants,

but tonight she's watching a good movie.

but this evening I'm going to bed early.

but today he's eating at a restaurant.

but today she's wearing a bright red dress.

but today you're wearing a skirt.

but he normally drinks beer.

but today I'm walking as my car won't start.

but this morning he's having eggs.

but this year we're visiting Italy.

but today he's wearing a business suit.

but she usually works in an office.

3.5 CROSS OUT THE INCORRECT WORD IN EACH SENTENCE

They ~~isn't~~ / aren't wearing coats.

❶ Vlad isn't / aren't playing soccer.

❷ We isn't / aren't working today.

❸ Manek isn't / aren't wearing a tie.

❹ We isn't / aren't coming to the party.

❺ Clarice isn't / aren't having dinner today.

❻ Jonathan isn't / aren't walking the dog.

❼ Mark and Trevor isn't / aren't going to the theater.

❽ Pedro isn't / aren't wearing a suit.

❾ Sally and Clive isn't / aren't going on vacation.

❿ Sebastian isn't / aren't watching the movie.

⓫ You isn't / aren't working hard enough.

 3.6 WRITE EACH SENTENCE IN ITS OTHER FORM

Karl is writing.	Karl isn't writing.
❶ Angelica is watching TV.	
❷	I'm not working at home.
❸ We're playing soccer.	
❹	Ginny isn't eating a burger.
❺ Sharon is listening to music.	
❻	They aren't drinking soda.
❼ We're going shopping.	
❽	Anita isn't visiting Athens.
❾ Pete's playing tennis.	
❿	You aren't speaking Dutch.
⓫ Paul's wearing a hat.	
⓬	I am not walking home.
⓭ Steven is going swimming.	

3.7 REWRITE THE SENTENCES, PUTTING THE WORDS IN THE CORRECT ORDER

wearing   Greg   isn't   a   suit.

Greg isn't wearing a suit.

1. on   going   this   vacation   year.   Kate   isn't

2. walk.   is   the   dog   Tracy   for   a   taking

3. isn't   Irena   to   party.   coming   the

4. walking   We   to   today.   school   are

5. cooking   Trevor   dinner.   his   is

6. traveling   Mr. Smith   is   Singapore.   to

7. today.   playing   aren't   soccer   They

8. a   am   pair   of   shoes.   I   buying   new

9. aren't   coat   a   You   today.   wearing

3.8 MARK THE SENTENCES THAT MATCH THE PICTURES

Deborah is wearing a hat. ✓
Deborah isn't wearing a hat. ☐

1. Jenny is wearing a red dress. ☐
   Jenny is wearing pants. ☐

2. Gemma is driving to work. ☐
   Gemma isn't driving to work. ☐

3. We are dancing. ☐
   We are singing. ☐

4. Brendan is eating a burger. ☐
   Brendan isn't eating a burger. ☐

5. Sal is wearing a short coat. ☐
   Sal is wearing a long coat. ☐

6. Mo is reading a book. ☐
   Mo is watching a movie. ☐

7. Emily is wearing glasses. ☐
   Emily is wearing a scarf. ☐

8. Jo is speaking on her cellphone. ☐
   Jo is listening to music. ☐

9. Kate is wearing jeans. ☐
   Kate is wearing a skirt. ☐

21

04 What's happening?

You can use the present continuous to ask about things that are happening now, in this moment, or today.

⚙ **New language** Present continuous questions
Aa Vocabulary Activities and gadgets
🧩 **New skill** Asking about the present

4.1 MATCH THE QUESTIONS TO THEIR ANSWERS

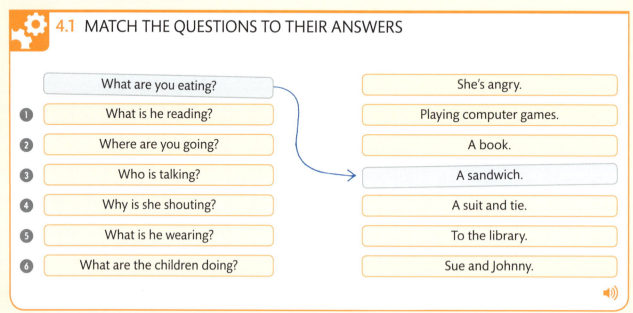

What are you eating?

1 What is he reading?
2 Where are you going?
3 Who is talking?
4 Why is she shouting?
5 What is he wearing?
6 What are the children doing?

She's angry.

Playing computer games.

A book.

A sandwich.

A suit and tie.

To the library.

Sue and Johnny.

4.2 FILL IN THE GAPS USING THE WORDS IN THE PANEL

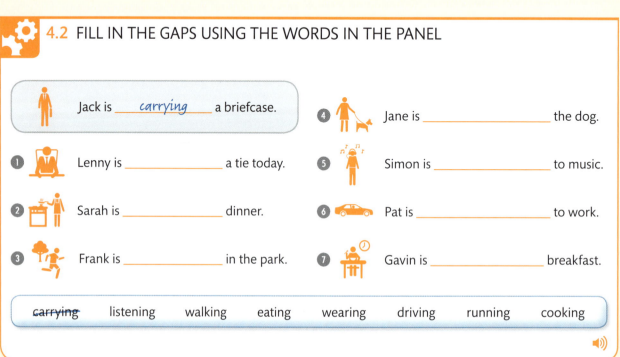

Jack is ___carrying___ a briefcase.

1 Lenny is _____ a tie today.
2 Sarah is _____ dinner.
3 Frank is _____ in the park.

4 Jane is _____ the dog.
5 Simon is _____ to music.
6 Pat is _____ to work.
7 Gavin is _____ breakfast.

~~carrying~~   listening   walking   eating   wearing   driving   running   cooking

4.3 LISTEN TO THE AUDIO AND MATCH ACTIONS TO NAMES

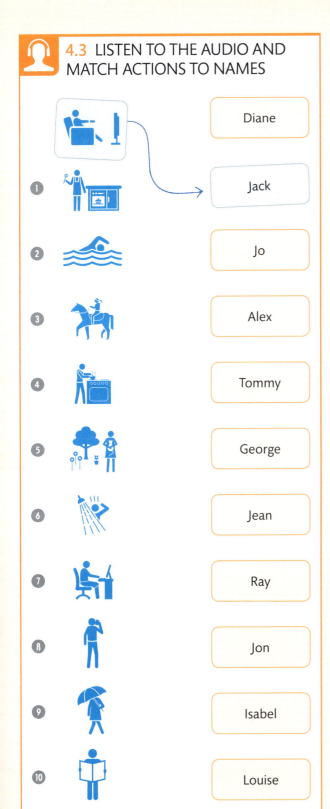

4.4 REWRITE THE SENTENCES, CORRECTING THE ERRORS

Jack and Mike **is watching** a film
Jack and Mike are watching a film.

1 I **are doing** my English homework.

2 He **is make** breakfast.

3 She **are reading** a magazine.

4 They **is running** by the river.

5 I **is writing** an email.

6 We **are listen** to music.

7 She **am driving** to London.

8 He **are taking** a bath.

9 They **are do** the shopping.

10 I **are eating** a pizza.

11 You **is riding** a motorcycle.

12 We **am going** to bed.

4.5 REWRITE THE SENTENCES AS QUESTIONS STARTING WITH "WHAT"

Jim is reading a book.
What is Jim reading?

1 Kay is watching a film.

2 Dan is eating spaghetti.

3 Tim and Jay are playing football.

4 Sara is wearing a dress.

5 You are carrying a suitcase.

6 Charlie is listening to his new CD.

7 Sharon is drinking water.

8 Sam is making a birthday cake.

9 You are writing an email.

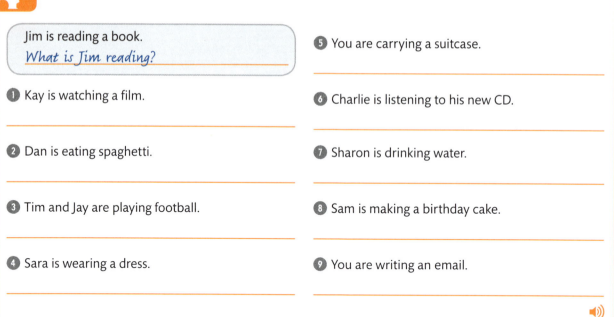

 4.6 REWRITE THE SENTENCES, PUTTING THE WORDS IN THE CORRECT ORDER

| drawing? | is | What | Jack |

What is Jack drawing?

1 | going? | is | Kim | Where |

2 | you | are | Who | phoning? |

3 | crying? | are | Why | you |

4 | are | John? | meeting | When | you |

5 | cooking? | you | are | What |

6 | is | playing? | your band | Where |

7 | shouting? | you | Why | are |

8 | you | drinking? | are | What |

9 | are | the concert? | to | you | getting | How |

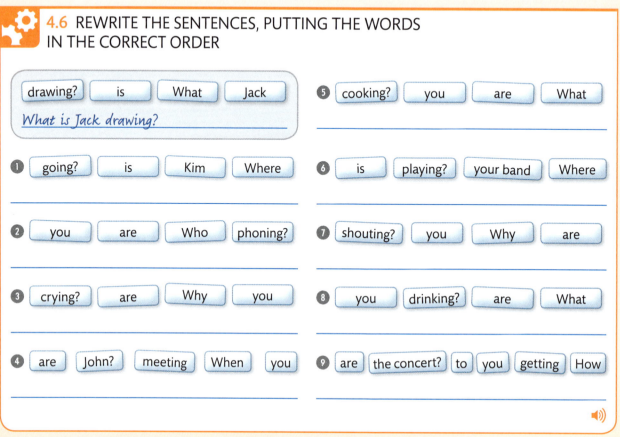

4.7 LISTEN TO THE AUDIO AND MATCH THE PRESENTS TO THE PEOPLE

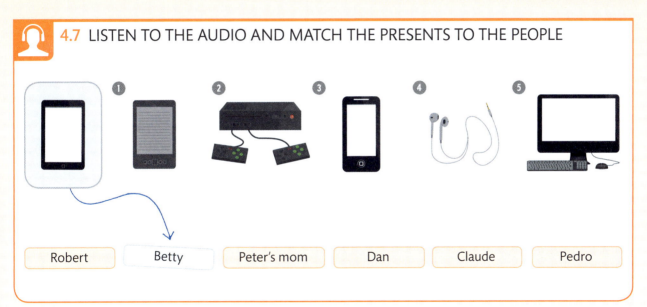

Robert   Betty   Peter's mom   Dan   Claude   Pedro

4.8 LOOK AT THE PICTURES, THEN RESPOND OUT LOUD TO THE AUDIO

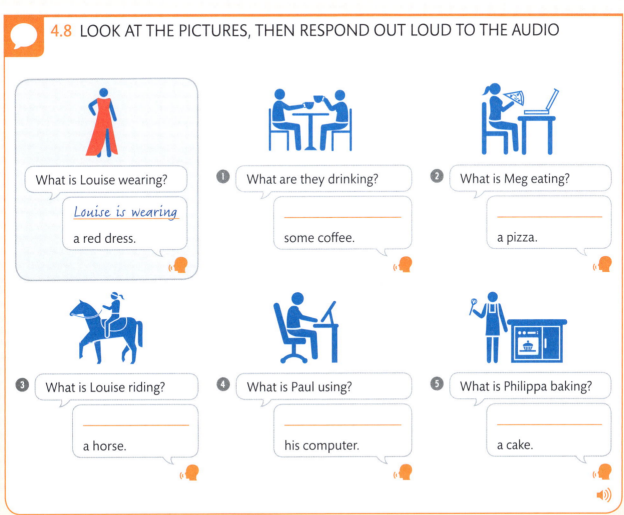

What is Louise wearing?

Louise is wearing a red dress.

① What are they drinking?

_____ some coffee.

② What is Meg eating?

_____ a pizza.

③ What is Louise riding?

_____ a horse.

④ What is Paul using?

_____ his computer.

⑤ What is Philippa baking?

_____ a cake.

Types of verbs

You can use most verbs in the continuous form to describe ongoing actions. Some verbs cannot be used in this way. These are called "state" verbs.

⚙ **New language** Action and state verbs
Aa Vocabulary Activities
New skill Using state verbs

5.1 WRITE THE WORDS FROM THE PANEL IN THE CORRECT GROUPS

ACTION VERBS

read
_____
_____
_____
_____

STATE VERBS

like
_____
_____
_____
_____

eat   ~~like~~   have

sing   learn

~~read~~   love

want   play

remember

go   listen

know   hate

5.2 SAY THE SENTENCES OUT LOUD, CORRECTING THE ERRORS

Suzy is knowing Jim.

Suzy knows Jim.

❶ I am remembering it is your birthday today.

❷ Dan is wanting a drink.

❸ You are having two sisters.

❹ He is owning this house.

❺ My brother is loving Anne.

❻ We are owning a horse.

❼ My dad is hating pizza.

5.3 CROSS OUT THE INCORRECT WORDS IN EACH SENTENCE

 I **want** / ~~am wanting~~ some juice please.

1 Greg **plays** / **is playing** tennis now.

2 Mo **watches** / **is watching** TV right now.

3 We **have** / **are having** a new dog.

4 You **don't like** / **aren't liking** snakes.

5 Dom **goes** / **is going** to school now.

 5.4 LISTEN TO THE AUDIO AND FILL IN THE GAPS

Jane is talking about her life in Los Angeles and her family.

Jane ___*lives*___ in Los Angeles.

1 Jane _____ at the school near her apartment.

2 Jane really _____ teaching.

3 Jane _____ to restaurants on the weekend.

4 Jane _____ three children.

5 Ben _____ soccer with his friends.

6 Silvia _____ a film at the movie theater.

7 Mike _____ to music in his room.

Aa **5.5 MATCH THE PICTURES TO THE CORRECT SENTENCES**

She hates snakes.

He's watching TV.

Samantha has three children.

She's listening to music.

They're running to school.

06 Vocabulary

Aa 6.1 FEELINGS AND MOODS WRITE THE WORDS FROM THE PANEL UNDER THE CORRECT PICTURES

happy

1 _____

2 _____

3 _____

6 _____

7 _____

8 _____

9 _____

12 _____

13 _____

14 _____

15 _____

18 _____

19 _____

20 _____

21 _____

4 _____

5 _____

10 _____

11 _____

16 _____

17 _____

22 _____

23 _____

relaxed   angry

disappointed   ~~happy~~

irritated   proud

scared   calm

surprised   distracted

confused   lonely

unhappy   excited

grateful   stressed

tired   anxious

bored   worried

jealous   confident

curious   amused

07 How are you feeling?

Talking about your feelings is an important part of everyday conversation. Use the present continuous to talk about how you're feeling.

⚙ **New language** "Feeling" and emotions
Aa Vocabulary Adjectives of emotions
✣ **New skill** Talking about your feelings

Aa **7.1** FIND THE 10 EMOTION ADJECTIVES IN THE GRID

```
N S A B I N E R V O U S L X N G O Q H N V
R D E M O S M D S C A L M R S M D T M A R D
S I N T E R P I U T C U D E R A I I T P U I
E K A T E B E A R X I N P E B A D R S P N G
M E X C I T E D F L A N G R Y A K E I Y N C
P T L S L C A Z I O R P L E A S E D L R I O
```

| excited | nervous | bored | pleased | bad | calm | happy | sad | angry | tired |

7.2 CROSS OUT THE INCORRECT WORD IN EACH SENTENCE

We are feeling confident / **nervous**.

 ❶ Alexander is feeling **excited** / calm.

 ❷ Danny is feeling **tired** / cheerful.

 ❸ Peter is feeling anxious / **proud**.

 ❹ Samantha is feeling **happy** / sad.

 ❺ I'm feeling miserable / **happy**.

 ❻ Christopher is feeling sad / **curious**.

 ❼ Waldo is feeling happy / **bored**.

7.3 MATCH THE PICTURES TO THE CORRECT SENTENCES

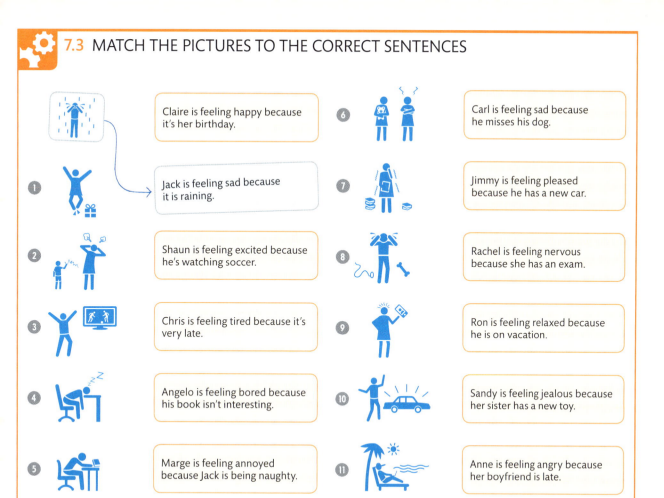

Claire is feeling happy because it's her birthday.

1 Jack is feeling sad because it is raining.

2 Shaun is feeling excited because he's watching soccer.

3 Chris is feeling tired because it's very late.

4 Angelo is feeling bored because his book isn't interesting.

5 Marge is feeling annoyed because Jack is being naughty.

6 Carl is feeling sad because he misses his dog.

7 Jimmy is feeling pleased because he has a new car.

8 Rachel is feeling nervous because she has an exam.

9 Ron is feeling relaxed because he is on vacation.

10 Sandy is feeling jealous because her sister has a new toy.

11 Anne is feeling angry because her boyfriend is late.

7.4 USE THE CHART TO CREATE 12 CORRECT SENTENCES AND SAY THEM OUT LOUD

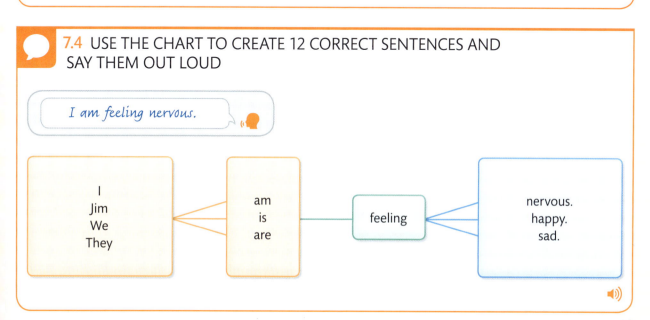

I am feeling nervous.

| I / Jim / We / They | am / is / are | feeling | nervous. / happy. / sad. |

Several people are telling their friends how they feel today.

Tammy is feeling...
nervous. ☐ happy. ☑ amused. ☐

5 Tanya is feeling...
irritated. ☐ tired. ☐ nervous. ☐

1 Charles is feeling...
scared. ☐ bored. ☐ angry. ☐

6 Bill and Susan are feeling...
excited. ☐ scared. ☐ nervous. ☐

2 Colin is feeling...
tired. ☐ sad. ☐ happy. ☐

7 Giles is feeling...
happy. ☐ nervous. ☐ furious. ☐

3 Jim is feeling...
nervous. ☐ sad. ☐ angry. ☐

8 Arnold is feeling...
tired. ☐ angry. ☐ relaxed. ☐

4 Greg is feeling...
tired. ☐ sad. ☐ annoyed. ☐

9 Katy is feeling...
tired. ☐ bored. ☐ angry. ☐

7.6 MATCH THE SENTENCES THAT GO TOGETHER

Claude is feeling really happy today.

So he's staying in bed.

1 Evie is really angry.

He didn't win the competition.

2 Peter is feeling very tired today.

He wants something to do.

3 Jenny is so nervous.

It's his birthday.

4 Danny is feeling really disappointed.

The bus still hasn't arrived.

5 Angelo is so bored.

She has an exam tomorrow.

I have my exam tomorrow. It's science, and I'm not very good at it. I'm so _____ *nervous* _____ .

③ I don't know what to do. There's nothing on TV. I'm really _____ .

① It's my birthday tomorrow. I really can't wait! I'm so _____ .

④ This book is really depressing. So many bad things happen. I'm feeling really _____ .

② I don't like this house. It's so dark. Is that a spider? I'm feeling very _____ .

⑤ My girlfriend's forgotten my birthday. And she forgot last year. I'm so _____ .

| angry | ~~nervous~~ | scared | sad | excited | bored |

Vocabulary

Aa **8.1 TRANSPORTATION** WRITE THE WORDS FROM THE PANEL
UNDER THE CORRECT PICTURES

bicycle

1 _____

2 _____

3 _____

8 _____

9 _____

10 _____

11 _____

16 _____

17 _____

18 _____

19 _____

20 _____

21 _____

22 _____

23 _____

4 _____

5 _____

6 _____

7 _____

12 _____

13 _____

14 _____

15 _____

taxi	steering wheel	walk	taxi rank
plane	ticket	bus stop	ride a bike
road	car	train	fly a plane
boat	yacht	port	tram
~~bicycle~~	bus	helicopter	fare
airport	drive a car	ship	train station

Routines and exceptions

Use the present simple to describe routines, and the present continuous to say what you are doing now. These tenses are often used together.

⚙ **New language** Exceptions
Aa Vocabulary Time markers
🧩 **New skill** Contrasting routines and exceptions

⚙ **9.1** FILL IN THE GAPS BY PUTTING THE VERBS IN THE CORRECT TENSES

Doug usually ___orders___ (order) a pizza on Fridays, but today he ___is cooking___ (cook).

1 Tony often _____ (go) for a swim in the evening, but today he _____ (visit) a friend.

2 Today Baz _____ (have) eggs, but he mostly _____ (eat) cereal for breakfast.

3 John's sister usually _____ (drive) to work, but today she _____ (walk).

4 Clara usually _____ (sleep) in the afternoon, but today she _____ (go) for a walk.

5 My cousins often _____ (play) soccer together, but today they _____ (play) golf.

6 He normally _____ (go) on vacation to Peru, but this year he _____ (visit) Greece.

7 Jenny usually _____ (watch) TV in the evening, but tonight she _____ (read).

8 Abe often _____ (play) soccer on Fridays, but today he _____ (watch) a game.

9 Tonight our dog _____ (sleep) in the kitchen, but he often _____ (sleep) outside.

10 Liza usually _____ (go) to the gym after work, but today she _____ (rest).

11 They often _____ (go) running on Saturdays, but today they _____ (shop).

9.2 REWRITE THE SENTENCES, CORRECTING THE ERRORS

> Sam usually is playing tennis on Thursdays, but today he play golf with his brother.
> *Sam usually plays tennis on Thursdays, but today he is playing golf with his brother.*

1 My wife usually worked until 5pm, but this evening she working until 7:30pm.

_____

2 Jim often is listening to the radio in the evening, but tonight he go to a party.

_____

3 I often meeting my friends in the evening, but tonight I meets my grandmother.

_____

4 Mrs. Brown teaches English this week, but she normally was teaching geography.

_____

5 Hank walk in the Pyrenees this week, but he usually going to work every day.

_____

9.3 SAY THE SENTENCES OUT LOUD, PUTTING THE VERBS IN THE CORRECT TENSES

> Mike ___*is wearing*___ (wear) a T-shirt today, but he normally ___*wears*___ (wear) a suit.

1 I normally _____ (go) to bed at 11pm, but tonight I _____ (meet) some friends.

2 Today Jane _____ (eat) a sandwich, but she often _____ (have) soup for lunch.

3 Sam usually _____ (drink) coffee, but this morning he _____ (drink) tea.

4 Tonight we _____ (have) water with our dinner, but we usually _____ (have) juice.

5 I usually _____ (feel) confident about exams, but today I _____ (feel) nervous.

Vocabulary

Aa **10.1 THE BODY** WRITE THE WORDS FROM THE PANEL
UNDER THE CORRECT PICTURES

mouth

1 _____

2 _____

3 _____

4 _____

8 _____

9 _____

10 _____

11 _____

12 _____

16 _____

17 _____

18 _____

19 _____

20 _____

24 _____

25 _____

26 _____

27 _____

28 _____

5 _____

6 _____

7 _____

13 _____

14 _____

15 _____

21 _____

22 _____

23 _____

29 _____

30 _____

31 _____

lips   chest

eye   nose   arm

eyebrow   head

ankle   toes

cheek   shoulders   shin

neck   foot

stomach   fingers

fingernail   thumb

hair   chin   leg

eyelashes   tooth

heel   face   teeth

knee   hand

knuckles   ~~mouth~~

thigh   ear

11 What's the matter?

There are many different ways to say you're sick. You often use the negative, "not well," to talk about general illness, and "hurts," "ache," or "pain" for specific problems.

⚙ **New language** Health complaints
Aa Vocabulary Body parts and pain phrases
🧩 **New skill** Saying what's wrong

 11.1 REWRITE THE SENTENCES, CORRECTING THE ERRORS

> Doug is not **feel** very well today, so he is not coming to work.
> _Doug is not feeling very well today, so he is not coming to work._

❶ I **don't** feeling well today. I'm sorry. Let's meet next week instead.

_____

❷ May and Clara are **feel** sick today. They're going to stay at home.

_____

❸ Cathy **not** feeling well. She is not going swimming today.

_____

❹ Jerry is **feel** really sick, but he's still going to work.

_____

❺ We don't **feeling** well, so we aren't coming to the party tonight.

_____

❻ Alexander **not** feel well. He's going to stay at home today.

_____

❼ They don't **feeling** well. They're not going to visit their uncle and aunt today.

_____

❽ Hilary isn't **feels** well. She can't come to the movies tonight.

_____

❾ Lee **feel** sick. He can't come to the sales meeting today.

_____

❿ John and Diana **is** not feeling well. They are going to leave work early today.

_____

🔊

11.2 FILL IN THE GAPS USING THE WORDS IN THE PANEL

Fiona has an awful _toothache_ .

① I can't hear and I have an _____ .

② Dan's leg _____ .

③ Maria has a _____ leg.

④ I don't feel well. I have a _____ .

⑤ Claire has a terrible _____ .

⑥ I have a _____ in my knee.

⑦ Philip can't stand. He has _____ .

stomachache	headache	pain	broken
hurts	~~toothache~~	backache	earache

11.3 LISTEN TO THE AUDIO AND ANSWER THE QUESTIONS

Alfred is visiting Dr. McCloud and telling him about his health problems.

Alfred's back is hurting.
True ✔ False ☐ Not given ☐

① Alfred's legs hurt.
True ☐ False ☐ Not given ☐

② His arm is hurting.
True ☐ False ☐ Not given ☐

③ Alfred's arm is broken.
True ☐ False ☐ Not given ☐

④ He has a pain in his shoulder.
True ☐ False ☐ Not given ☐

⑤ Alfred has a pain in his foot.
True ☐ False ☐ Not given ☐

⑥ Alfred has a toothache.
True ☐ False ☐ Not given ☐

⑦ He has a headache.
True ☐ False ☐ Not given ☐

11.4 USE THE CHART TO CREATE 12 CORRECT SENTENCES AND SAY THEM OUT LOUD

I have a broken leg.

I / You / Anna	have / has / have got	a broken leg. / a pain in my foot. / a headache.

Aa 12.1 WEATHER WRITE THE WORDS FROM THE PANEL UNDER THE CORRECT PICTURES

warm

1 _____

2 _____

3 _____

8 _____

9 _____

10 _____

11 _____

16 _____

17 _____

18 _____

19 _____

20 _____

21 _____

22 _____

23 _____

4  _____

5  _____

6  _____

7  _____

12  _____

13  _____

14  _____

15  _____

cloud	hot	snow	flood
freezing	humidity	cold	rainbow
blue sky	hail	thunder	puddle
wet	tornado	boiling	gale
~~warm~~	lightning	wind	ice
rain	sun	temperature	dry

13 What's the weather like?

There are many ways to talk about the weather.
Use the verb "to be" with weather words and phrases
to describe the temperature and conditions.

⚙ **New language** Weather descriptions
Aa **Vocabulary** Temperature words
🧩 **New skill** Talking about the weather

Aa 13.1 MATCH THE PICTURES TO THE DESCRIPTIONS

It's a sunny day and there's lots of snow. It's perfect weather for skiing.

The weather is wonderful here. It's sunny, and we're having a nice time.

The weather here is very stormy. Last night we had lots of lightning.

It's freezing here. It's too cold to stay outdoors for very long.

There were icicles on the house this morning. It's very cold here.

It's boiling here. It's too hot to go out in the middle of the day.

It's a really windy day here. I'm going windsurfing later today.

The weather here is horrible! It's raining all the time. It's cold and wet.

⚙ 13.2 WRITE EACH SENTENCE IN ITS OTHER FORM

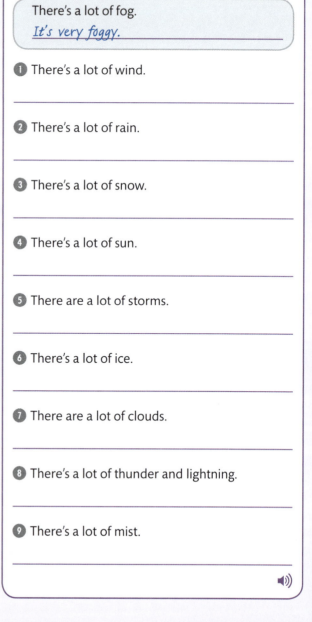

There's a lot of fog.
It's very foggy.

1 There's a lot of wind.

2 There's a lot of rain.

3 There's a lot of snow.

4 There's a lot of sun.

5 There are a lot of storms.

6 There's a lot of ice.

7 There are a lot of clouds.

8 There's a lot of thunder and lightning.

9 There's a lot of mist.

13.3 FILL IN THE GAPS USING THE WORDS IN THE PANEL

It's _____boiling_____ here in Morocco. It's 104°F.

❶ Be careful. There's _____ on the road.

❷ The weather's beautiful. It's hot and _____ .

❸ It's quite _____ here. The temperature is 68°F.

❹ It's 14°F here and it's snowy. It's _____ .

❺ Oh no, it's _____ . We can't play tennis now.

❻ It's very _____ . The airport is closed.

❼ There's a _____ . We can't play golf.

| warm | freezing | ice | foggy | ~~boiling~~ | raining | storm | sunny |

13.4 LISTEN TO THE AUDIO AND ANSWER THE QUESTIONS

A radio presenter is describing the weather across Europe.

Where is it sunny?
Northern Europe ☐ **Central Europe** ☑

❶ Where is it not raining?
Britain ☐ **Spain** ☐ **Germany** ☐

❷ Which is the coldest city in Europe?
London ☐ **Copenhagen** ☐ **Berlin** ☐

❸ Which is the hottest city in Europe?
Madrid ☐ **Rome** ☐ **Lisbon** ☐

❹ Where should you not drive?
Italy ☐ **Finland** ☐ **Sweden** ☐

❺ Where will there be no clouds?
Britain ☐ **Scandinavia** ☐ **France** ☐

13.5 USE THE CHART TO CREATE 10 CORRECT SENTENCES AND SAY THEM OUT LOUD

There's a lot of rain at the moment.

| There's / It's | a lot of really quite | rain / sun / warm / freezing | at the moment. / in London today. |

14 Vocabulary

Aa **14.1 TRAVEL** WRITE THE WORDS FROM THE PANEL UNDER THE CORRECT PICTURES

stay in a hotel

1 _____

2 _____

3 _____

6 _____

7 _____

8 _____

9 _____

12 _____

13 _____

14 _____

15 _____

18 _____

19 _____

20 _____

21 _____

④ _____

⑤ _____

⑩ _____

⑪ _____

⑯ _____

⑰ _____

㉒ _____

㉓ _____

leave a hotel   luggage

security   road trip

hand luggage   runway

on time   passport control

miss a flight   board a plane

~~stay in a hotel~~   reception

apartment   pack your bags

late   arrive at the airport

boarding card   hostel

arrive at a hotel   get on a bus

fly in a plane   go sightseeing

get off a bus   cruise

🔊

47

15 Making comparisons

A comparative adjective is used to describe the difference between two nouns. Use it before the word "than" to compare people, places, or things.

🔧 **New language** Comparative adjectives
Aa Vocabulary Travel and countries
🧩 **New skill** Comparing things

15.1 FILL IN THE GAPS USING THE WORDS IN THE PANEL

The bag is bigger than the _watch_ .

1 I'm _____ than you are.

2 A train is _____ than a bus.

3 79°F is _____ than 64°F.

4 A car is faster than a _____ .

5 _____ is smaller than Russia.

6 Everest is higher than _____ .

7 6am is _____ than 9am.

8 A tiger is _____ than a pig.

9 Your dress is _____ than mine.

10 95°F is _____ than 110°F.

11 The Sahara is _____ than the Arctic.

12 11pm is _____ than 3pm.

13 An _____ is bigger than a mouse.

14 A plane is _____ than a car.

15 _____ is colder than milk.

16 Mars is _____ to Earth than Pluto.

17 Athens is _____ than Los Angeles.

France	later	taller	bigger	ice cream	bike
hotter	~~watch~~	colder	Mont Blanc	older	faster
prettier	hotter	earlier	faster	elephant	closer

🔊

Aa 15.2 FIND EIGHT COMPARATIVE ADJECTIVES IN THE GRID AND WRITE THEM DOWN

```
V D I H O T T E R I T V
I H R L L U W L O W E R
B E Q R X D I R T I E R
I C A O L A T E R H Z X
G L Z S Y F Y B I C D P
G G R Y I T H I N N E R
E Q Z T T E L A R G E R
R U V I B N R L V Q G R
```

1. thin   =   *thinner*
2. easy   =   _____
3. late   =   _____
4. dirty   =   _____
5. large   =   _____
6. big   =   _____
7. hot   =   _____
8. low   =   _____

15.3 FILL IN THE GAPS BY PUTTING THE ADJECTIVES IN THEIR COMPARATIVE FORM

Platinum is very **expensive**. It's _____ *more expensive than* _____ gold.

1. This painting is **beautiful**. It's _____ that one.

2. Russian is very **difficult**. It's _____ Italian.

3. Rome is very **old**. It's _____ my city.

4. Pizza is very **tasty**. It's _____ pasta.

5. China is very **large**. It's _____ Germany.

6. Oslo is very **cold**. It's _____ Paris.

7. Science is very **difficult**. It's _____ geography.

8. Monaco is very **expensive**. It's _____ Berlin.

9. Mountain climbing is **dangerous**. It's _____ hiking.

10. This book is very **interesting**. It's _____ yours.

11. Skiing is **exciting**. It's _____ jogging.

15.4 LISTEN TO THE AUDIO AND ANSWER THE QUESTIONS

Dave is calling a travel agent to book a vacation.

Sicily is more expensive than Greece.
True ☑   False ☐

❶ The resort in Greece is bigger.
True ☐   False ☐

❷ The resort in Sicily is more interesting.
True ☐   False ☐

❸ The beaches in Sicily are more beautiful.
True ☐   False ☐

❹ Dave thinks Greek food is tastier.
True ☐   False ☐

❺ Sicily is hotter than Greece.
True ☐   False ☐

15.5 FILL IN THE GAPS BY PUTTING THE ADJECTIVES INTO THE COMPARATIVE FORM

Nine o'clock is _____*later than*_____ (late) seven o'clock.

Seven o'clock is _____*earlier than*_____ (early) nine o'clock.

❶ Flying is _____ (safe) driving.

Driving is _____ (dangerous) flying.

❷ My computer is _____ (old) my phone.

My phone is _____ (new) my computer.

❸ The suitcase is _____ (heavy) the bag.

The bag is _____ (light) the suitcase.

❹ This champagne is _____ (expensive) that wine.

This wine is _____ (cheap) that champagne.

❺ 118°F is _____ (hot) 90°F.

90°F is _____ (cold) than 118°F.

15.6 SAY THE SENTENCES OUT LOUD, FILLING IN THE GAPS WITH COMPARATIVE PHRASES

A horse _____ *is bigger than* _____ (big) a dog.

1. 11pm _____ (late) 10pm.

2. Gold _____ (cheap) platinum.

3. Athens _____ (old) Los Angeles.

4. Chess _____ (difficult) poker.

5. Tennis _____ (energetic) walking.

15.7 SAY THE SENTENCES OUT LOUD, FILLING IN THE GAPS WITH COMPARATIVE PHRASES

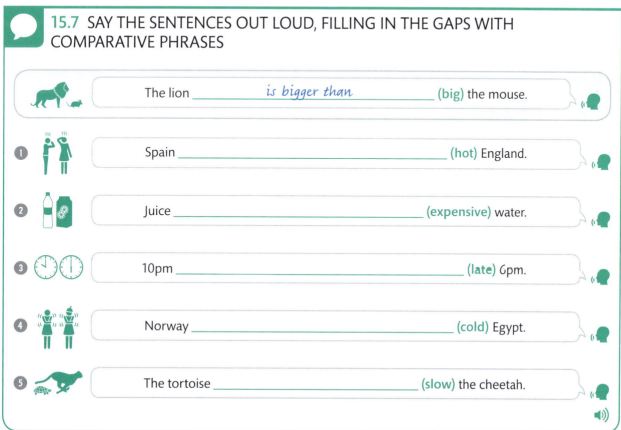

The lion _____ *is bigger than* _____ (big) the mouse.

1. Spain _____ (hot) England.

2. Juice _____ (expensive) water.

3. 10pm _____ (late) 6pm.

4. Norway _____ (cold) Egypt.

5. The tortoise _____ (slow) the cheetah.

16 Talking about extremes

Use superlative adjectives to talk about extremes, such as "the biggest" or "the smallest." For long adjectives, use "the most" to make the superlative.

⚙ **New language** Superlative adjectives
Aa Vocabulary Animals, facts, and places
🧩 **New skill** Talking about extremes

⚙ **16.1 FILL IN THE GAPS BY PUTTING THE ADJECTIVES IN THEIR SUPERLATIVE FORM**

Death Valley in California is the _____*hottest*_____ (hot) place in the world.

1 The Great Wall of China is the _____ (long) wall in the world.

2 The African Bush Elephant is the _____ (big) land animal.

3 Vatican City is the _____ (small) country in the world.

4 The Burj Khalifa is the _____ (tall) building in the world.

5 The Amazon is the _____ (wide) river in the world.

6 Dolphins are in the top 10 _____ (intelligent) animals.

🔊

⚙ **16.2 WRITE THE SUPERLATIVE FORM OF EACH ADJECTIVE**

	high	*highest*	8	ugly	
1	small		9	clean	
2	big		10	dirty	
3	far		11	expensive	
4	high		12	new	
5	thin		13	old	
6	fat		14	intelligent	
7	beautiful		15	fast	

16.3 LISTEN TO THE AUDIO AND ANSWER THE QUESTIONS

Jane, Sue, and Dan are talking about their cars and phones.

Who has the newest car?
Dan ☐ Jane ☐ Sue ☑

① Who has the fastest car?
Dan ☐ Jane ☐ Sue ☐

② Who has the biggest car?
Dan ☐ Jane ☐ Sue ☐

③ Who has the most comfortable car?
Dan ☐ Jane ☐ Sue ☐

④ Who has the newest phone?
Dan ☐ Jane ☐ Sue ☐

⑤ Who is the safest driver?
Dan ☐ Jane ☐ Sue ☐

⑥ Who drives the farthest?
Dan ☐ Jane ☐ Sue ☐

⑦ Who is the most experienced driver?
Dan ☐ Jane ☐ Sue ☐

16.4 FILL IN THE GAPS USING THE SUPERLATIVE FORM OF THE ADJECTIVES IN THE PANEL

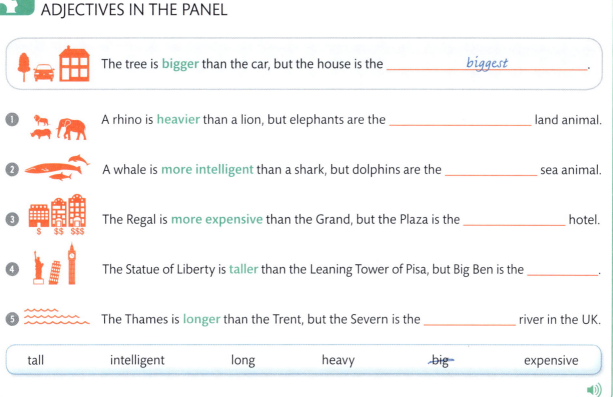

The tree is **bigger** than the car, but the house is the _____ *biggest* _____.

① A rhino is **heavier** than a lion, but elephants are the _____ land animal.

② A whale is **more intelligent** than a shark, but dolphins are the _____ sea animal.

③ The Regal is **more expensive** than the Grand, but the Plaza is the _____ hotel.

④ The Statue of Liberty is **taller** than the Leaning Tower of Pisa, but Big Ben is the _____.

⑤ The Thames is **longer** than the Trent, but the Severn is the _____ river in the UK.

| tall | intelligent | long | heavy | ~~big~~ | expensive |

16.5 WRITE THESE ADJECTIVES IN THEIR SUPERLATIVE FORMS

beautiful = *the most beautiful*

1 expensive = _____

2 comfortable = _____

3 intelligent = _____

4 dangerous = _____

5 exciting = _____

6 impressive = _____

7 handsome = _____

16.6 READ THE BLOG AND ANSWER THE QUESTIONS

Which is the most expensive hotel?
The Rialto ☐ The Plaza ☐ The Grand ✓

1 Which hotel is closest to the city center?
The Rialto ☐ The Plaza ☐ The Grand ☐

2 Which is the biggest hotel?
The Rialto ☐ The Plaza ☐ The Grand ☐

3 Which hotel provides the best breakfast?
The Rialto ☐ The Plaza ☐ The Grand ☐

4 Which is the most historic hotel?
The Rialto ☐ The Plaza ☐ The Grand ☐

5 Which is the newest hotel?
The Rialto ☐ The Plaza ☐ The Grand ☐

6 Which hotel has rooms with the most impressive views?
The Rialto ☐ The Plaza ☐ The Grand ☐

Best Hotels

HOME | ENTRIES | ABOUT | CONTACT

THE TOP THREE

The Rialto
This hotel is perfect for a city break because it is right in the city center. It has 100 rooms and has been a hotel since 1925. Some rooms come with an impressive view of the castle. Rooms cost from $120 a night for a double, with a simple continental breakfast included.

The Plaza
This is a new hotel, with 80 rooms. The hotel attracts lots of business people as well as tourists. It is famed for having the best breakfast in the city. Rooms cost from $150 a night for a double.

The Grand
This is officially the oldest hotel in the city, so it has lots of history. With 120 rooms it is one of the biggest hotels in the city. Rooms cost from $180 a night for a double.

16.7 REWRITE THE SENTENCES, CORRECTING THE ERRORS

The older cave paintings in the world are about 40,000 years old.
The oldest cave paintings in the world are about 40,000 years old.

1 The Amazon rainforest has some of the more beautiful plants in the world.

_____

2 Mesopotamia is thought to be the home of the earlier civilization in the world.

_____

3 The British Museum is the more popular tourist attraction in the UK.

_____

4 New York City and Geneva are the more expensive cities in the world.

_____

5 Hippopotamuses are one of the world's more dangerous animals.

_____

16.8 SAY THE SENTENCES OUT LOUD, FILLING IN THE GAPS WITH SUPERLATIVES

Moscow is a very large city. It is _____ *the largest city* _____ in Europe.

1 The Shanghai Tower is a very tall building. It is _____ in China.

2 The sloth is a very slow animal. It is _____ in the world.

3 The Vasco da Gama bridge in Portugal is very long. It is _____ in Europe.

4 The Dead Sea is a very low point on Earth. It is _____ on Earth.

5 Mount Elbrus in Russia is a very tall mountain. It is _____ in Europe.

17 Vocabulary

sand dune

① _____

② _____

③ _____

⑧ _____

⑨ _____

⑩ _____

⑪ _____

⑯ _____

⑰ _____

⑱ _____

⑲ _____

ocean	rocks	coast	swamp
countryside	~~sand dune~~	river	polar region
volcano	iceberg	beach	waterfall

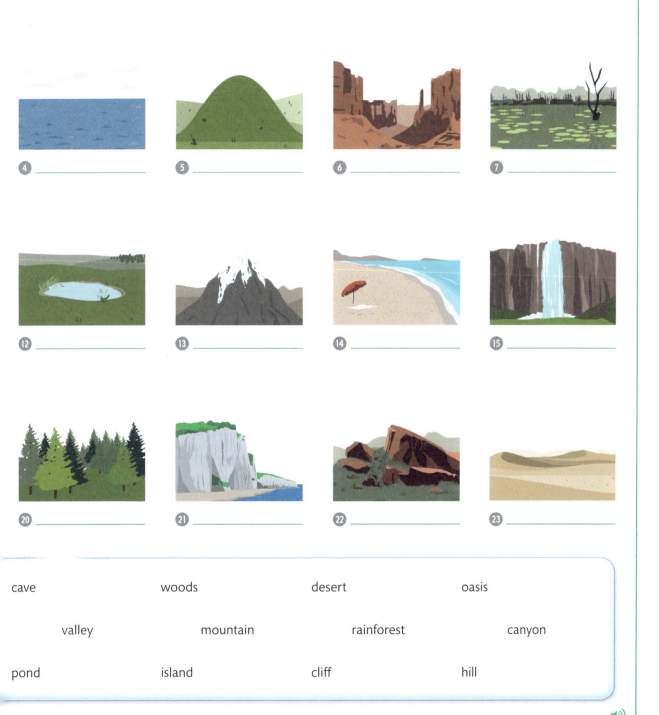

4 _____

5 _____

6 _____

7 _____

12 _____

13 _____

14 _____

15 _____

20 _____

21 _____

22 _____

23 _____

cave   woods   desert   oasis

   valley   mountain   rainforest   canyon

pond   island   cliff   hill

18 Making choices

"Which," "what," "and," and "or" are all useful words to add to questions. You can use them to show whether a question is general or about specific options.

⚙ **New language** "Which" and "what"
Aa Vocabulary Geographical words
🧩 **New skill** Asking multiple-choice questions

⚙ **18.1 CROSS OUT THE INCORRECT WORD IN EACH SENTENCE**

 Would you like a burger and / ~~or~~ soda for lunch?

① Would you like to stay in and / or watch a DVD tonight?

② Do you want to go to the Tower of London and / or the London Eye?

③ Do you want pizza and / or salad for dinner tonight?

④ Is Marianne a pop singer and / or a modern jazz singer?

⑤ Can I pay for the washing machine in cash and / or by credit card?

⑥ On birthdays, we open our presents and / or play party games.

⑦ Do you want to go to a movie and / or the theater tomorrow night?

⑧ Would you like to study French and / or German next year?

⑨ Did you live in a house and / or an apartment when you were in Thailand?

⑩ I had coffee and / or chocolate cake at the new café in town.

⑪ Would you like tea and / or coffee while you wait for your appointment?

18.2 MARK THE SENTENCES THAT ARE CORRECT

Which is the tallest building in Asia? ☐
What is the tallest building in Asia? ☑

1 What is Tom's car, the red or the blue one? ☐
Which is Tom's car, the red or the blue one? ☐

2 What is the biggest country in Europe? ☐
Which is the biggest country in Europe? ☐

3 What is bigger, a lion or a hippo? ☐
Which is bigger, a lion or a hippo? ☐

4 What would you like? Cake or cookies? ☐
Which would you like? Cake or cookies? ☐

5 What would you like to do this evening? ☐
Which would you like to do this evening? ☐

6 What shall we have for dinner tonight? ☐
Which shall we have for dinner tonight? ☐

7 What ink does he use, black or blue? ☐
Which ink does he use, black or blue? ☐

8 What is your favorite food? ☐
Which is your favorite food? ☐

9 What is the tallest mountain in the world? ☐
Which is the tallest mountain in the world? ☐

🔊

18.3 FILL IN THE GAPS USING "WHICH" OR "WHAT"

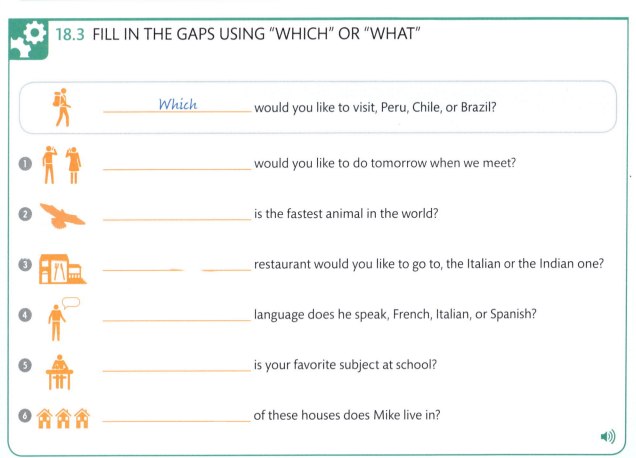

___Which___ would you like to visit, Peru, Chile, or Brazil?

1 _____ would you like to do tomorrow when we meet?

2 _____ is the fastest animal in the world?

3 _____ restaurant would you like to go to, the Italian or the Indian one?

4 _____ language does he speak, French, Italian, or Spanish?

5 _____ is your favorite subject at school?

6 _____ of these houses does Mike live in?

🔊

59

18.4 FILL IN THE GAPS USING THE COMPARATIVE OR SUPERLATIVE FORM OF THE ADJECTIVES

Anna is _____*better*_____ (good) at skiing than I am.

1. My exam results were _____ (bad) than Frank's.

2. The Plaza is the _____ (good) hotel in the city.

3. My new workplace is _____ (far) from my house than my old one.

4. I am a _____ (good) driver than my brother.

5. Don't go to Gigi's. It's the _____ (bad) café in town.

6. Neptune is the _____ (far) planet from the Sun.

18.5 COMBINE THE TWO SENTENCES TO MAKE ONE SENTENCE, THEN SAY IT OUT LOUD

I am good at tennis. My sister is better.

My sister _____*is better at*_____ *tennis than I am.*_____

1. I am bad at soccer. My brother is worse.

My brother is _____ _____

2. The red T-shirt is $10. The blue T-shirt is $15.

The blue T-shirt is _____ _____

3. Gino's café is good. Harry's café is better.

Harry's cafe is _____ _____

4. My sister isn't good at languages. I am worse.

I am _____ _____

5. The red pen is $7. The blue one is $5.

The blue pen is _____ _____

18.6 READ THE POSTCARD AND WRITE ANSWERS TO THE QUESTIONS AS FULL SENTENCES

Which city is more expensive, Paris or Rome?

Paris is more expensive than Rome.

❶ Which is better, the food in Paris or at home?

_____

❷ Where did Pat eat the best meal?

_____

❸ What is the tallest building in Paris?

_____

❹ Where can you hear the best music in Paris?

_____

❺ What's the most famous painting in the Louvre?

_____

Dear Kim,
Bonjour! Paris is much more expensive than Rome. The food here is much better than at home. I had the best meal ever at La Coupole last night. I visited the Eiffel Tower on the weekend. Did you know it's the tallest building in the city? I went to Le Pompon on Thursday. It has the best music in Paris. On Sunday I went to the Louvre. There is a lot there, but its most famous painting is the Mona Lisa.
Love,
Pat

18.7 SAY THE SENTENCES OUT LOUD, FILLING IN THE GAPS

Anna _____ *is the best* _____ (good) driver in her family.

❶ Rhode Island _____ (small) state in the US.

❷ The Humber Bridge _____ (long) than the Severn Bridge.

❸ George _____ (bad) student in the class.

❹ A Ferrari _____ (expensive) than a Fiat car.

❺ Saturn _____ (far) from Earth than Mars.

You usually write numbers larger than 100 in figures. To say them, add "and" in front of the number signified by the last two digits, such as "one hundred and ten."

⚙ **New language** Large numbers
Aa Vocabulary Thousands and millions
✦ **New skill** Talking about large amounts

19.1 LISTEN TO THE AUDIO AND MARK THE NUMBERS YOU HEAR

513 ✓
530 ☐

① 8,426 ☐
8,624 ☐

② 3,499,000 ☐
3,495,000 ☐

③ 469,236 ☐
496,632 ☐

④ 3,735,000 ☐
3,573,000 ☐

⑤ 50,275 ☐
15,265 ☐

⑥ 1,537,895 ☐
1,357,985 ☐

19.2 SAY THE NUMBERS OUT LOUD

532 — *five hundred and thirty-two*

① 7,396

② 34,975

③ 212,457

④ 15,795,000

⑤ 26,655,872

⑥ 47,229,286

⑦ 53,198,538

19.3 WRITE THE NUMBERS USING NUMERALS

Five million, two thousand, seven hundred and fifty-six = 5,002,756

1 Four hundred and fifty-five thousand and fifty-eight = _____

2 Five hundred and sixty-four thousand, one hundred and forty-three = _____

3 Three thousand, six hundred and eighty-two = _____

4 Forty-five million, seven hundred and twelve thousand, six hundred = _____

5 Sixty-three thousand, eight hundred and fifty-nine = _____

6 Nine hundred and fifty thousand, eight hundred and thirty-seven = _____

7 Twenty-three million, one hundred thousand, two hundred and sixty-nine = _____

8 Nine hundred and seventy-eight = _____

9 One hundred and eighty-five thousand, seven hundred and ninety-four = _____

10 Fifty million, two hundred and twelve thousand, seven hundred and five = _____

11 Ten million, four hundred and sixty thousand, two hundred and forty = _____

12 Three hundred and thirty-six thousand, four hundred and twenty-two = _____

13 Sixteen thousand, seven hundred and three = _____

14 One million, three hundred and fifty-nine thousand, six hundred and seven = _____

◄))

19.4 LISTEN TO THE AUDIO AND WRITE THE NUMBERS YOU HEAR

73,245

5 _____   10 _____

1 _____   6 _____   11 _____

2 _____   7 _____   12 _____

3 _____   8 _____   13 _____

4 _____   9 _____   14 _____

20 Vocabulary

Aa **20.1 THE CALENDAR** WRITE THE WORDS FROM THE PANEL UNDER THE CORRECT PICTURES

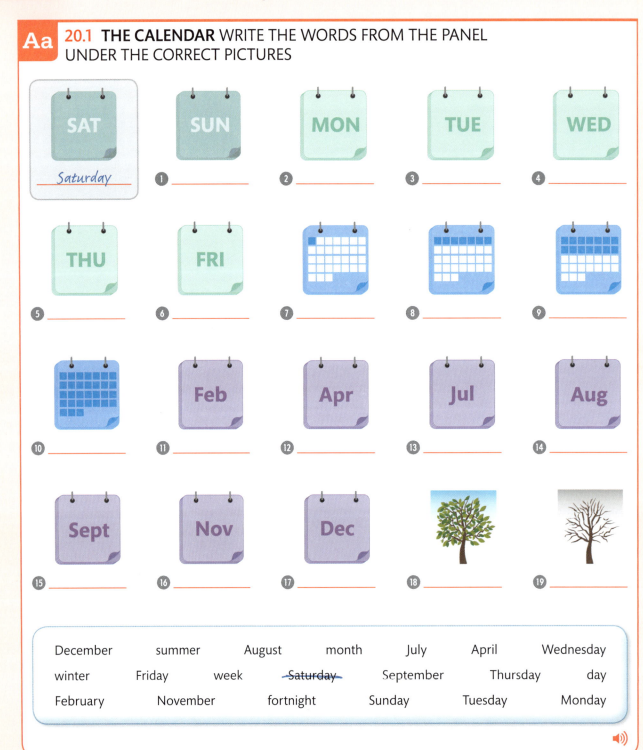

SAT — Saturday

SUN — 1 _____

MON — 2 _____

TUE — 3 _____

WED — 4 _____

THU — 5 _____

FRI — 6 _____

7 _____

8 _____

9 _____

10 _____

Feb — 11 _____

Apr — 12 _____

Jul — 13 _____

Aug — 14 _____

Sept — 15 _____

Nov — 16 _____

Dec — 17 _____

18 _____

19 _____

December	summer	August	month	July	April	Wednesday
winter	Friday	week	~~Saturday~~	September	Thursday	day
February	November	fortnight	Sunday	Tuesday	Monday

20.2 ORDINAL NUMBERS WRITE THE WORDS FROM THE PANEL UNDER THE CORRECT NUMBERS

2nd
second

19th
① _____

26th
② _____

5th
③ _____

6th
④ _____

29th
⑤ _____

21st
⑥ _____

16th
⑦ _____

27th
⑧ _____

17th
⑨ _____

10th
⑩ _____

14th
⑪ _____

1st
⑫ _____

11th
⑬ _____

20th
⑭ _____

23rd
⑮ _____

31st
⑯ _____

7th
⑰ _____

3rd
⑱ _____

4th
⑲ _____

---

second   twenty-third   twenty-ninth   twenty-seventh

twenty-first   ninteenth   twenty-sixth   thirty-first   fifth   seventh

seventeenth   twentieth   tenth   sixteenth   first

third   eleventh   fourth   fourteenth   sixth

🔊

21 Talking about dates

There are two different ways of writing and saying dates. You use numbers along with the month to define the date you're talking about.

⚙️ **New language** Dates, "was born," "ago"
Aa Vocabulary Numbers, months, and years
🧩 **New skill** Talking about dates

21.1 WRITE EACH SENTENCE IN ITS OTHER FORM

TIP
Write dates in the form "May 2" in US English, but "the 2nd of May" in UK English.

Sally arrives on the 4th of August.	*Sally arrives on August 4.*

1. _____ | We returned on September 9.
2. Sarah was born on the 12th of March. | _____
3. _____ | Greg was born on February 12.
4. My birthday is on the 22nd of November. | _____
5. _____ | I stop working on July 21.
6. The year begins on the 1st of January. | _____

21.2 LISTEN TO THE AUDIO AND ANSWER THE QUESTIONS

Claire and Phil are discussing a suitable date for meeting.

On November 23, Claire...
- **is meeting a colleague.** ☐
- **is meeting a client.** ☑
- **is not at work.** ☐

❶ On November 24, Phil...
- **is not at work.** ☐
- **has another meeting.** ☐
- **is visiting the factory.** ☐

❷ On November 25, Claire...
- **is going to Seattle.** ☐
- **is on vacation.** ☐
- **is going to Los Angeles.** ☐

❸ On November 26, Phil...
- **is free all day.** ☐
- **is busy all day.** ☐
- **is in Los Angeles.** ☐

21.3 READ THE ARTICLE AND ANSWER THE QUESTIONS

Clarissa was born in 1980.
True ☐ False ☐ Not given ✓

① She was born in New York City.
True ☐ False ☐ Not given ☐

② Clarissa became famous in the 1980s.
True ☐ False ☐ Not given ☐

③ Heaven's Child released five albums.
True ☐ False ☐ Not given ☐

④ Her first album was called *Clarissa*.
True ☐ False ☐ Not given ☐

⑤ She released *Clarissa* in 2012.
True ☐ False ☐ Not given ☐

⑥ She has released a perfume.
True ☐ False ☐ Not given ☐

⑦ She was 25 when she married a singer.
True ☐ False ☐ Not given ☐

Singing sensation

Clarissa's rise to fame

Clarissa was born in New York City in 1985. She is one of the most successful singers in the world. She became famous in the 1990s when she started singing professionally.

Her first solo album was *Carried Away*. Clarissa released it in 2005, when she was 20 years old. The album won lots of awards, including five Best Singer of the Year Awards. She has released seven more albums, including *Clarissa* in 2012, which sold 15 million copies.

Clarissa has starred in lots of movies, and played a singer in *Supergirls* in 2006. She also released a perfume in 2012.

She married a singer in 2008, when she was 23. They had a child in 2011.

21.4 USE THE CHART TO CREATE EIGHT CORRECT SENTENCES AND SAY THEM OUT LOUD

My wedding is on February 16.

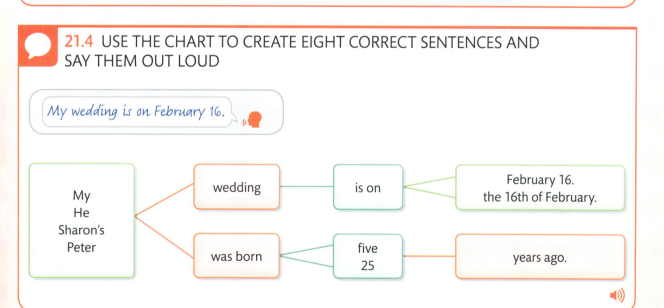

| My / He / Sharon's / Peter | wedding | is on | February 16. / the 16th of February. |
| | was born | five / 25 | years ago. |

22 Talking about the past

The past simple describes events that happened at a definite time in the past, or the state of things at a particular point in time.

⚙ **New language** The past simple of "to be"
Aa Vocabulary Jobs, town, and life events
🧩 **New skill** Talking about past states

22.1 CROSS OUT THE INCORRECT WORD IN EACH SENTENCE

You ~~was~~ / were at the museum this afternoon.

1 Roberta was / were at the party last night.

2 We was / were in college together.

3 You was / were a student at that time.

4 There was / were lots of people in town.

5 They was / were there in the evening.

6 Your friends was / were at the museum yesterday.

7 She was / were a teacher in the 1970s.

8 There was / were a café near the beach.

9 My mom was / were a dentist.

10 Chris and I was / were happy about the news.

11 They was / were at the theater last night.

12 Frank was / were an actor in the 1990s.

13 It was / were very cold in Norway.

14 My parents was / were away last week.

15 We was / were in Los Angeles in 2014.

16 You was / were at the movie theater on Friday.

17 Jenny was / were a nurse for 20 years.

22.2 LISTEN TO THE AUDIO AND MATCH THE YEARS TO THE CORRECT EVENTS

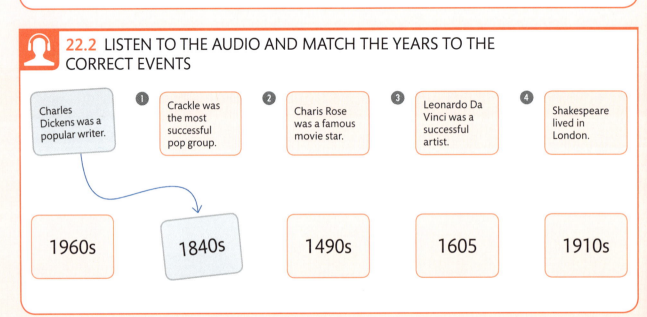

Charles Dickens was a popular writer.

1 Crackle was the most successful pop group.

2 Charis Rose was a famous movie star.

3 Leonardo Da Vinci was a successful artist.

4 Shakespeare lived in London.

1960s

1840s

1490s

1605

1910s

22.3 READ THE EMAIL AND ANSWER THE QUESTIONS

To: Mick

Subject: My trip to Dublin

Hi Mick,

How are you? I was in Dublin last week with my friend Janet. It's a beautiful city. You should visit some day!
We were at Dublin Castle. Do you know it? It's very old, and was built in 1204. The weather wasn't so good while we were there. It was cold and it rained a lot. There were lots of people there, though!
We were on Grafton Street where there were lots of stores, and some nice cafes, too. When we were in a traditional Irish bar, I drank some Guinness.
On Friday, we were at the Botanical Gardens. It was so beautiful there.

See you soon,
Cath

		True	False
	Cath was in Dubai last weekend.	☐	✔
❶	Cath was in Dublin with her friend Jane.	☐	☐
❷	She visited the cathedral.	☐	☐
❸	Dublin Castle was built in 1204.	☐	☐
❹	The weather was bad.	☐	☐
❺	There weren't many people.	☐	☐
❻	There were museums on Grafton Street.	☐	☐
❼	They were in an Irish bar.	☐	☐
❽	Cath drank Guinness in Dublin.	☐	☐
❾	They were at Dublin Zoo.	☐	☐
❿	On Thursday, they were at the Botanical Gardens.	☐	☐

22.4 CROSS OUT THE INCORRECT WORD IN EACH SENTENCE

They ~~wasn't~~ / weren't very good at science.

1 It wasn't / weren't an interesting book.

2 There wasn't / weren't any good movies on.

3 We wasn't / weren't in the US in 2012.

4 Glen wasn't / weren't at home when I called.

5 There wasn't / weren't a theater in my town.

6 Trevor wasn't / weren't in Berlin in 1994.

7 There wasn't / weren't a library in the town.

8 We wasn't / weren't at home last night.

9 Peter wasn't / weren't a student at Harvard.

10 Carlo wasn't / weren't very good at singing.

11 Meg and Clive wasn't / weren't teachers then.

12 They wasn't / weren't at the restaurant last night.

🔊

22.5 WRITE EACH SENTENCE IN ITS NEGATIVE FORM

She was a very good teacher.
She wasn't a very good teacher.

1 Brad was a teacher in 2012.

_____

2 The weather was bad.

_____

3 It was a comfortable bed.

_____

4 They were interesting people.

_____

5 Brendan's parents were doctors.

_____

6 Pete and Sue were on the beach all day.

_____

🔊

22.6 REWRITE THE SENTENCES, PUTTING THE WORDS IN THE CORRECT ORDER

| weren't | There | cafés. | good | any |

There weren't any good cafés.

1 | 30 | was | Simon | an actor | years. | for |

_____

2 | was | really | It | in | Canada. | cold |

_____

3 | the | town? | there | any | in | Were | stores |

4 | dancing. | Phil | at | good | wasn't |

5 | Rebecca | in | Was | in | 2010? | Arizona |

🔊

70

22.7 SAY QUESTIONS TO MATCH THE STATEMENTS, SPEAKING OUT LOUD

They were late for the English lesson.

Were they late for the English lesson?

⑤ James was at work until 8 o'clock yesterday.

① She was at school in the nineties.

⑥ You were at the airport before me.

② You were at the park last Sunday.

⑦ They were at Simon's wedding last week.

③ There were lots of people at his party.

⑧ We were in Spain for two weeks.

④ He was very good at playing soccer.

⑨ Hayley was happy in college.

22.8 USE THE CHART TO CREATE NINE CORRECT QUESTIONS AND SAY THEM OUT LOUD

Was she a teacher?

| Was Were | she they there you | a teacher? angry? a party last night? at home yesterday? |

23 Past events

Some verbs are regular in the past simple. You can use a lot of them to talk about the past week, the last year, or your life. Their past simple forms ends in "-ed."

⚙ **New language** Regular verbs in the past simple
Aa **Vocabulary** Pastimes and life events
🧩 **New skill** Talking about your past

⚙ **23.1 FILL IN THE GAPS BY PUTTING THE VERBS IN THE PAST SIMPLE**

Gary ___played___ (play) soccer last night.

❶ Roger _____ (watch) the game.

❷ They _____ (call) their dad yesterday.

❸ We _____ (arrive) at the hotel at 7pm.

❹ They _____ (walk) to school yesterday.

❺ Simon _____ (work) late last week.

❻ My mother _____ (dance) at the party.

❼ They _____ (wash) their new car.

❽ Terry _____ (study) French at school.

❾ Karen _____ (travel) to Africa.

🔊

⚙ **23.2 FILL IN THE GAPS TO WRITE THE OPPOSITE OF EACH SENTENCE**

I **cooked** dinner last night.	_I didn't cook dinner last night._
❶ _____	Craig didn't **phone** his girlfriend.
❷ The doctor **visited** my grandmother.	_____
❸ _____	We didn't **play** tennis last night.
❹ My sister **walked** to the shops.	_____
❺ _____	They didn't **watch** TV last night.
❻ Debbie **moved** to the US this year.	_____
❼ _____	David didn't **clean** his room again.

23.3 FILL IN THE GAPS USING THE WORDS IN THE PANEL

Chris _____danced_____ at the party.

1 Kelly _____ TV last night.

2 Tim _____ home on Friday.

3 Ed _____ as a waiter last year.

4 I _____ some Mexican food.

5 Marge _____ her sister last night.

6 Marion _____ some music.

7 The children _____ a question.

8 My dad _____ in Canada.

9 They _____ my birthday.

worked	remembered	asked	played	lived
walked	watched	tried	~~danced~~	called

Aa **23.4 FIND NINE PAST SIMPLE VERBS IN THE GRID AND LIST THEM ACCORDING TO THEIR SPELLING RULES**

```
E L S T A R T E D A M A T
Y Q F V R E Z C S E O E A
E M S N K V R A N R V C C
A R R I V E D L Y F E H V
O V L N E R X K T P D Z R
G E A W A S H E D D N S L
R D O R V T G F Q V I Z E
O A I C N U Y Y E I B T K
N N D I M D E M S S A S E
O C A R R I E D E I A S J
G E E I E E D R M T T O W
A D R E H D L G O E M N A
A G I D X R K R C D O A R
```

VERBS THAT TAKE "ED"

1 _washed_

2 _____

3 _____

VERBS THAT TAKE "IED"

4 _studied_

5 _____

6 _____

VERBS THAT TAKE "D"

7 _danced_

8 _____

9 _____

23.5 REWRITE THESE SENTENCES IN THE PAST SIMPLE

They **watch** TV together yesterday.
They watched TV together yesterday.

❶ I **study** English.

_____

❷ Jim **arrives** today.

_____

❸ My son **carries** my bags.

_____

❹ She **dances** very well.

_____

❺ Bill **washes** his socks.

_____

🔊

23.6 READ THE BLOG AND ANSWER THE QUESTIONS

On Monday, Zoe...
finished work early. ☐
worked late. ✓
watched a movie with her boyfriend. ☐

❶ On Tuesday, Zoe...
visited an old friend. ☐
cooked a delicious dinner. ☐
cleaned her kitchen. ☐

❷ On Tuesday evening, she...
watched TV with her boyfriend. ☐
listened to the radio. ☐
started a new book. ☐

❸ On Wednesday, she...
visited her grandmother. ☐
saw her friend and listened to music. ☐
painted the bathroom. ☐

❹ On Thursday, Zoe...
listened to the radio with a friend. ☐
danced at a party. ☐
washed the floors. ☐

Zoe's zone

HOME | ENTRIES | ABOUT | CONTACT

POSTED TUESDAY, MARCH 23

A BUSY WEEK

I'm sorry for not posting anything for a few days, but I was so busy last week.

On Monday, I worked at the restaurant until 1am. There was a big birthday party with lots of guests, and I only arrived home at 2am!

Tuesday was a bit better. I stayed at home and did some housework. I cleaned the kitchen and washed the floors. In the evening I watched a film on the TV with my boyfriend.

On Wednesday, I visited my grandmother. We walked by the river near her house. In the evening, she cooked a delicious dinner and we listened to some music.

On Thursday, my sister invited me to a party at her friend's. It was great. We danced all night!

23.7 LISTEN TO THE AUDIO AND MATCH THE BEGINNINGS OF THE SENTENCES TO THE CORRECT ENDINGS

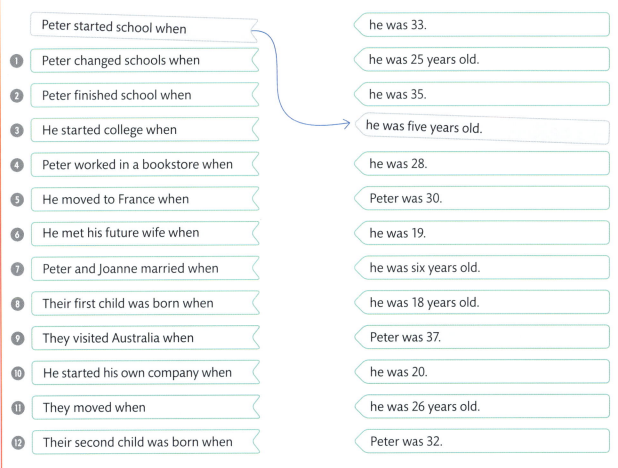

Peter started school when

1 Peter changed schools when

2 Peter finished school when

3 He started college when

4 Peter worked in a bookstore when

5 He moved to France when

6 He met his future wife when

7 Peter and Joanne married when

8 Their first child was born when

9 They visited Australia when

10 He started his own company when

11 They moved when

12 Their second child was born when

he was 33.

he was 25 years old.

he was 35.

he was five years old.

he was 28.

Peter was 30.

he was 19.

he was six years old.

he was 18 years old.

Peter was 37.

he was 20.

he was 26 years old.

Peter was 32.

23.8 USE THE CHART TO CREATE NINE CORRECT SENTENCES AND SAY THEM OUT LOUD

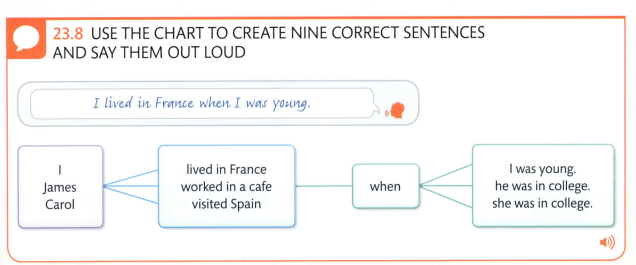

I lived in France when I was young.

| I James Carol | lived in France worked in a cafe visited Spain | when | I was young. he was in college. she was in college. |

24 Past abilities

In the past simple, "can" becomes "could." You often use it to talk about things you "could" do in the past, but can't do now.

 New language Using "could" in the past simple
Aa Vocabulary Abilities and pastimes
New skill Talking about past abilities

24.1 REWRITE THESE SENTENCES IN THE PAST TENSE USING "COULD"

Jimmy **can** cook Italian food. → *Jimmy could cook Italian food.*

1 Carl **can** run fast. _____

2 Brendan **can** speak five languages. _____

3 Sally **can** paint beautifully. _____

4 Rob and Sarah **can't** dance flamenco. _____

5 Yasmin **can** climb a tree. _____

6 Danny **can** drive a bus. _____

7 We **can't** ride a horse. _____

8 Jenny **can** play the violin. _____

9 Ben **can** fly a plane. _____

10 Yuna **can** speak Italian. _____

24.2 USE THE CHART TO CREATE 18 CORRECT SENTENCES AND SAY THEM OUT LOUD

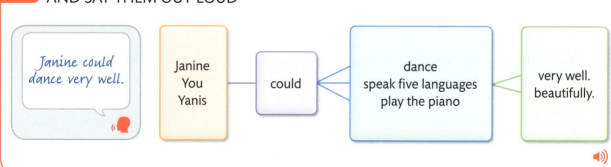

Janine could dance very well.

| Janine / You / Yanis | could | dance / speak five languages / play the piano | very well. / beautifully. |

Six people are talking about talents and skills.

When Sandra was one, she could...
walk. ✓
speak. ☐
read. ☐

3 When Max was young he could speak...
seven languages. ☐
six languages. ☐
five languages. ☐

1 Martha could play the violin when she was...
six. ☐
seven. ☐
eight. ☐

4 Winnie's grandmother could...
paint beautifully. ☐
bake cakes. ☐
dance salsa. ☐

2 James could paint well when he was...
three years old. ☐
seven years old. ☐
12 years old. ☐

5 When Alfie was a child he could...
climb a tree. ☐
climb a mountain. ☐
run very fast. ☐

24.4 REWRITE THE SENTENCES, PUTTING THE WORDS IN THE CORRECT ORDER

When · was · couldn't · swim. · I · five · I

When I was five I couldn't swim.

4 dog · very · could · My · quickly. · run

1 swim · was · Greg · when · he · four. · could

5 could · fluent · Greg · Russian. · speak

2 to · couldn't · the · come · party. · Simon

6 couldn't · I · the · snow. · because · of · drive

3 speak · could · Jean · Japanese.

7 find · street. · couldn't · We · your

25 Vocabulary

Aa **25.1 ENTERTAINMENT** WRITE THE WORDS FROM THE PANEL UNDER THE CORRECT PICTURES

movie star

1 _____

2 _____

3 _____

6 _____

7 _____

8 _____

9 _____

12 _____

13 _____

14 _____

15 _____

18 _____

19 _____

20 _____

21 _____

④ _____

⑤ _____

novel   TV show   bookstore

romance   horror

~~movie star~~   clap   science fiction

thriller   exhibition

play   documentary   author

newspaper   villain   movie

hero   action

musical   director   comedy

audience   crime

main character

⑩ _____

⑪ _____

⑯ _____

⑰ _____

㉒ _____

㉓ _____

26 Irregular past verbs

In the past simple, some verbs are irregular. Their past simple forms are not formed using the normal rules, and sometimes look very different from the infinitive forms.

⚙ **New language** Irregular verbs in the past simple
Aa Vocabulary Sequence words
🧩 **New skill** Describing the past

Aa 26.1 MATCH THE VERBS TO THEIR PAST FORMS

write → wrote

1. make — sang
2. sing — began
3. put — took
4. begin — made
5. meet — ate
6. sell — slept
7. take — put
8. eat — bought
9. see — met
10. sleep — saw
11. buy — sold

🔊

⚙ 26.2 FILL IN THE GAPS USING THE WORDS IN THE PANEL

Felicity _put_ the dishes in the cupboard.

1. Sophie _____ her cat to the vet.
2. I _____ you a letter. Did you get it?
3. We _____ some interesting people today.
4. Roger _____ a new car on Wednesday.
5. Jane _____ a really good film yesterday.
6. I _____ a postcard from my brother.
7. Derek _____ home at 11pm.
8. Archie _____ a cake for my birthday.
9. My son _____ school yesterday.
10. I _____ my glasses under the bed.
11. Sid _____ happy when he finished school.
12. Bobby _____ a song to his mother.

put̶	saw	began
found	met	wrote
bought	sang	felt	made
got	went	took

🔊

80

Selma ___broke___ (break) the classroom window while playing with her friends.

❶ Samantha and Cathy _____ (eat) pizza after work.

❷ Katy _____ (go) to the disco with Ben on Friday night.

❸ Miguel _____ (write) a beautiful song about his wife Christine.

❹ Pauline and Emma _____ (get) lots of presents for Christmas this year.

❺ The kids _____ (see) a play at the theater with us last week.

❻ Keith _____ (buy) a new guitar for his brother Patrick on his birthday.

❼ Emily _____ (sleep) in a tent in the back yard last night.

❽ Pablo _____ (sing) a traditional song at Elma and Mark's wedding.

❾ Tammy _____ (sell) her old computer to her neighbor Anna.

❿ They _____ (feel) sad after watching the film about a boy who lost his dog.

⓫ Mick _____ (begin) to read a new book yesterday evening.

⓬ Joan _____ (find) a gold necklace in the garden while she was gardening.

⓭ We _____ (take) the children to the movie theater next to the shopping mall.

⓮ Warren _____ (make) a delicious sandwich for his daughter's lunch.

26.4 FILL IN THE GAPS USING THE WORDS IN THE PANEL

I had a shower. _____*Then*_____ I had breakfast with my family.

❶ _____ , Bob ate some soup. Then he had a burger and a sandwich.

❷ My cousins have stayed for six weeks! They've _____ decided to go home.

❸ First, I went to the baker's. _____ , I went to the butcher's next door.

❹ Samantha gave me a letter. _____ , she left to go back home.

first	next	~~then~~	finally	after that

🔊

Aa 26.5 MATCH THE QUESTIONS TO THEIR ANSWERS

Did you go to the party?   Yes, he's really handsome.

❶ Did Samantha take her money?   No, it was too expensive.

❷ Did you get some bread?   Yes, I had a great time.

❸ Did you meet Rebecca's boyfriend?   No, the zoo was closed.

❹ Did you find your glasses?   No, there were no good movies on.

❺ Did you see any tigers?   Yes, he ate everything.

❻ Did Dan buy a new car?   Yes, we're moving on Saturday.

❼ Did you go to the movies?   No, it starts on Wednesday.

❽ Did Jim make that cake?   No, I sent him a text.

❾ Did Billy eat his dinner?   Sorry, the baker was closed.

❿ Did you write him a letter?   No, it was too noisy in my room.

⓫ Did you sell your house?   No, he bought it at the baker's.

⓬ Did you begin your course?   No, she left it on the table.

⓭ Did you sleep well?   Yes, they were in the bathroom.

🔊

82

26.6 REWRITE THE STATEMENTS AS SIMPLE QUESTIONS USING "DID"

They went to the beach by bus.

How *did they go to the beach?*

1 I saw a horror film at the movie theater.

What _____

2 Sarah took Phil to the wedding party.

Who _____

3 We had a pizza for dinner on Friday.

What _____

4 They went to New Zealand on vacation.

Where _____

5 Steve bought a new cellphone.

What _____

6 Jim ate fish and chips for lunch.

What _____

7 Kelly met her sister last week.

Who _____

8 Peter put his phone in the drawer.

Where _____

9 I found your watch in the garden.

Where _____

10 Anna made a sandwich for lunch.

What _____

11 I got a necklace from Doug.

What _____

12 Peter sang a rock song for Elma.

What _____

13 My sister came to see me yesterday.

When _____

Aa 26.7 WRITE THE VERBS IN THEIR PAST SIMPLE FORMS ON THE GRID

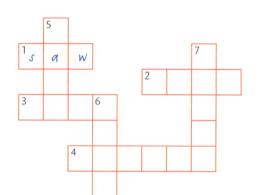

ACROSS

1 See

2 Sell

3 Feel

4 Buy

DOWN

5 Make

6 Take

7 Sleep

27 Vocabulary

Aa 27.1 **TOOLS** WRITE THE WORDS FROM THE PANEL UNDER THE CORRECT PICTURES

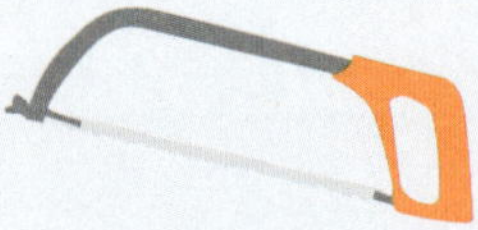

hacksaw

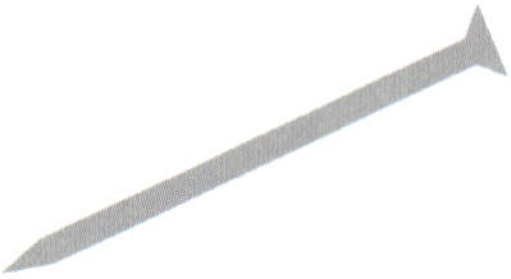

1 ______

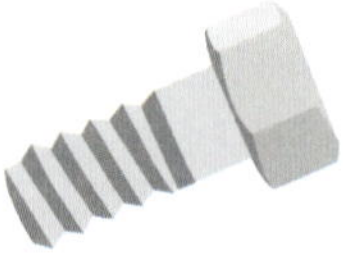

2 ______

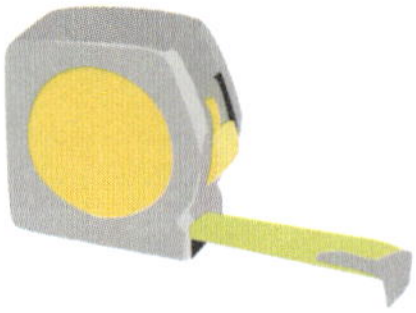

4 ______

5 ______

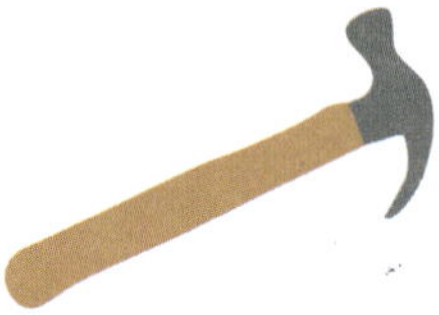

6 ______

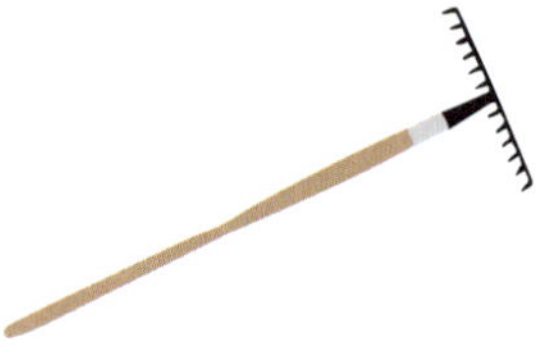

8 ______

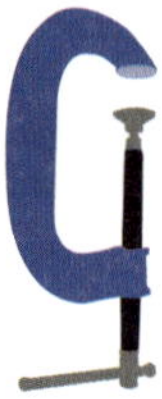

9 ______

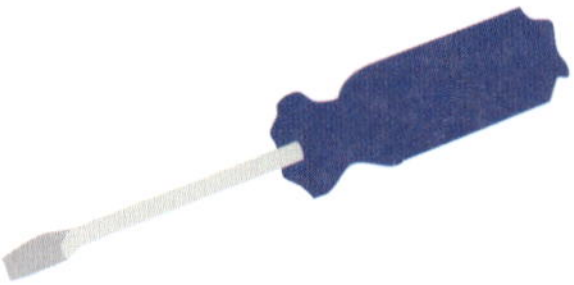

10 ______

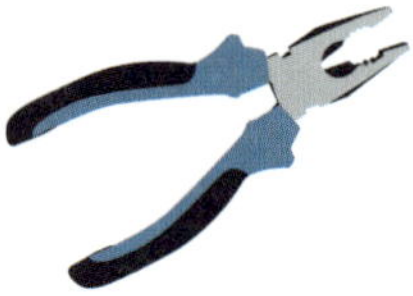

12 ______

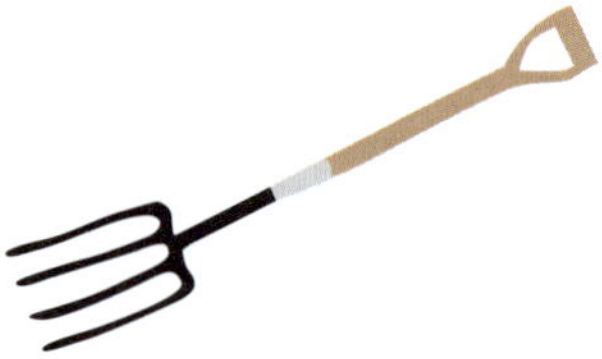

13 ______

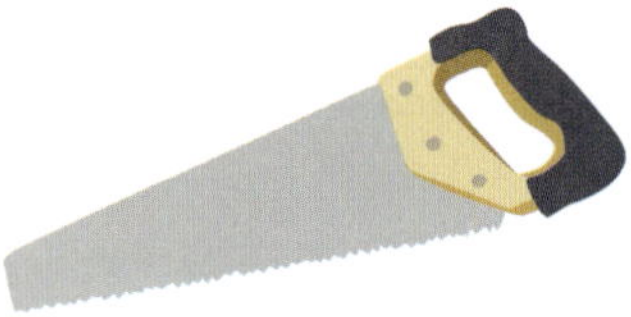

14 ______

tape measure, screw, clamp, hammer, bolt, saw, fork, pliers, drill, nail, screwdriver, trowel

3 _____

7 _____

11 _____

15 _____

nut   jigsaw

~~hacksaw~~   rake

27.2 KITCHEN IMPLEMENTS WRITE THE WORDS FROM THE PANEL UNDER THE CORRECT PICTURES

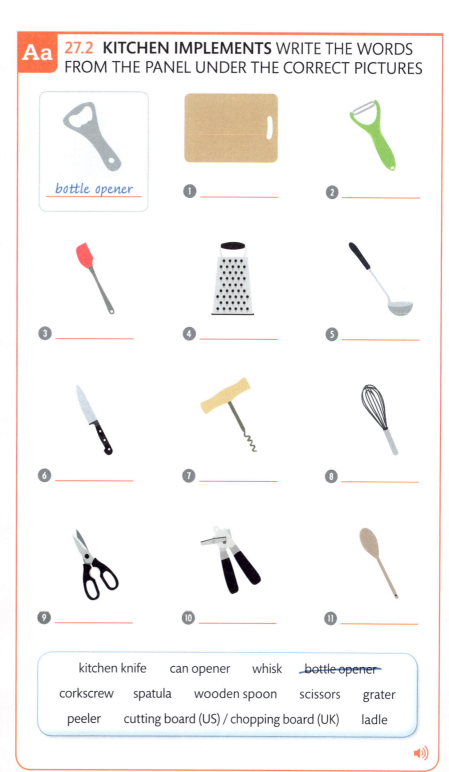

bottle opener

1 _____

2 _____

3 _____

4 _____

5 _____

6 _____

7 _____

8 _____

9 _____

10 _____

11 _____

kitchen knife   can opener   whisk   ~~bottle opener~~

corkscrew   spatula   wooden spoon   scissors   grater

peeler   cutting board (US) / chopping board (UK)   ladle

28 Telling a story

You can use "about" to describe the subject matter of movies, shows, and stories. Use adjectives to make a description more specific.

🔧 **New language** "About," opinions
Aa Vocabulary Opinions
🧩 **New skill** Describing media and culture

Aa 28.1 FIND SEVEN ADJECTIVES IN THE GRID AND WRITE THEM UNDER THE CORRECT HEADING

```
S  G  N  I  D  X  D  T  R  B
L  E  K  B  L  E  O  H  Y  O
O  D  R  M  J  A  J  R  S  R
W  K  N  S  I  Q  Y  I  R  I
F  U  N  N  Y  Y  E  L  B  N
E  D  I  S  R  B  R  L  Y  G
M  C  O  N  F  U  S  I  N  G
S  I  L  L  Y  N  S  N  N  V
E  X  C  I  T  I  N  G  N  D
```

POSITIVE OPINION

1. _funny_
2. _____
3. _____

NEGATIVE OPINION

4. _boring_
5. _____
6. _____
7. _____

Aa 28.2 MATCH THE PICTURES TO THE DESCRIPTIONS

It's a book about two young sisters from the country.

1. It's a thriller about two police officers.

2. It's a story about London in the 1890s.

3. It's a movie about a racing car driver.

4. It's a musical about a couple who got married.

5. It's a movie about two brothers.

🔊

28.3 READ THE FILM REVIEWS AND ANSWER THE QUESTIONS

 **Films on Friday**

HOME | ENTRIES | ABOUT | CONTACT

 Films out this Friday

Bankbreakers is a film about some friends who decide to rob a bank. They use the internet to find which banks in Europe hold the most money and valuable items. First they go to a bank in Munich, turn off the alarms, and steal some money and jewelry. After a successful robbery, the thieves decide to rob another bank in Paris. This time, they get caught by video surveillance cameras and they go to prison. I didn't enjoy the film. I thought it was a bit slow and not very well acted. *The King* is a film version of the Shakespeare play *Macbeth*. After a big battle, Macbeth meets three witches who tell him he will become Thane of Cawdor and then king. Although King Duncan gives Macbeth the title of Thane of Cawdor, Macbeth and his wife plot to kill him. I thought the film was thrilling because the story is exciting. I liked it a lot.

What is the film *Bankbreakers* about?

It's about some friends who rob a bank.

① Where is the first bank they rob?

_____

② How do they get into the first bank?

_____

③ How are the thieves caught?

_____

④ What happens to them after they are caught?

_____

⑤ What does the reviewer think of this film?

_____

⑥ What is the film *The King* based on?

_____

⑦ Who does Macbeth meet after a big battle?

_____

⑧ What does King Duncan give Macbeth?

_____

⑨ Who does Macbeth plot with?

_____

⑩ Who does Macbeth kill?

_____

⑪ What does the reviewer think of this film?

_____

28.4 LISTEN TO THE AUDIO AND NUMBER THE SENTENCES IN THE ORDER YOU HEAR THEM

Some friends are talking about books they have read, and films, plays, and musicals they have seen.

Ⓐ The play was about a hairdresser. ☐

Ⓑ The book was about some jewelry thieves. ☐

Ⓒ The couple in the film wanted a divorce. 1

Ⓓ The musical was called *Seven Days in Heaven*. ☐

Ⓔ The story is about an adventure kids went on. ☐

Ⓕ The film was about King George the Sixth. ☐

28.5 REWRITE THE SENTENCES, CORRECTING THE ERRORS

> I **enjoys** the play. It was thrilling.
> *I enjoyed the play. It was thrilling.*

❶ Jo **didn't enjoyed** the show because it was boring.

_____

❷ Hannah **didn't like** the film because it was fun.

_____

❸ I **hate** the musical because the story was silly.

_____

❹ He enjoyed the play because it was **thrilled**.

_____

❺ I **liked** the play because it was boring.

_____

❻ Paul hated the show because it was **scared**.

_____

❼ I **hates** the show because it was slow.

_____

❽ She liked the story because it was **romance**.

_____

❾ He **enjoys** the movie because it was exciting.

_____

❿ I hated the play because it was **bored**.

_____

⓫ He **doesn't enjoy** the film because it was scary.

_____

⓬ She liked the book because it was **excited**.

_____

⓭ I **don't like** the play because it was silly.

_____

⓮ The movie was **thrilled** and they loved it.

_____

⓯ I **enjoys** the musical because it was romantic.

_____

88

28.6 REWRITE THE SENTENCES, PUTTING THE WORDS IN THE CORRECT ORDER

funny. | I | opera | because | it | was | loved | the

I loved the opera because it was funny.

1. it | silly. | hated | musical | because | was | I | the

2. thrilling. | loved | film | was | Anna | it | the | because

3. the | Tom | it | didn't | slow. | movie | because | enjoy | was

4. it | enjoyed | because | the | was | Sam | film | funny.

5. because | a | Kay | book | had | it | romantic ending. | loved | the

6. the | boring. | was | hated | because | it | Jim | show

7. was | it | I | really liked | play | because | thrilling. | the

8. the | scary. | I | like | book | was | it | didn't | because

9. was | to understand. | it | didn't | the | because | difficult | I | enjoy | opera

10. the | had | enjoyed | because | story. | it | an | book | They | exciting

🔊

29 Asking about the past

You can make questions in the past simple using "did." This is useful for asking about past events, such as travel and vacations.

⚙️ **New language** Past simple questions
Aa Vocabulary Travel and activities
🧩 **New skill** Talking about vacations

29.1 REWRITE THE SENTENCES, PUTTING THE WORDS IN THE CORRECT ORDER

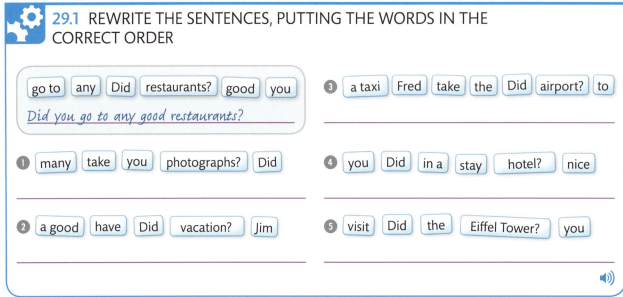

go to | any | Did | restaurants? | good | you

Did you go to any good restaurants?

1. many | take | you | photographs? | Did

_____

2. a good | have | Did | vacation? | Jim

_____

3. a taxi | Fred | take | the | Did | airport? | to

_____

4. you | Did | in a | stay | hotel? | nice

_____

5. visit | Did | the | Eiffel Tower? | you

_____

🔊

29.2 REWRITE THE SENTENCES AS QUESTIONS

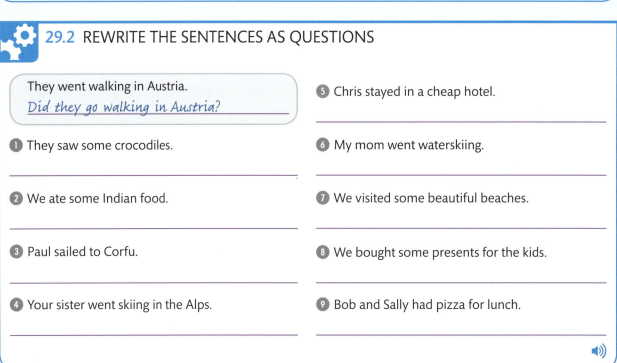

They went walking in Austria.
Did they go walking in Austria?

1. They saw some crocodiles.

_____

2. We ate some Indian food.

_____

3. Paul sailed to Corfu.

_____

4. Your sister went skiing in the Alps.

_____

5. Chris stayed in a cheap hotel.

_____

6. My mom went waterskiing.

_____

7. We visited some beautiful beaches.

_____

8. We bought some presents for the kids.

_____

9. Bob and Sally had pizza for lunch.

_____

🔊

29.3 LISTEN TO THE AUDIO AND MARK WHETHER EACH THING DID OR DIDN'T HAPPEN

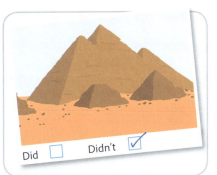

Did ☐   Didn't ☑

1 Did ☐   Didn't ☐

2 Did ☐   Didn't ☐

3 Did ☐   Didn't ☐

4 Did ☐   Didn't ☐

5 Did ☐   Didn't ☐

29.4 LISTEN TO THE AUDIO AGAIN AND ANSWER THE QUESTIONS WITH SHORT ANSWERS

Did Simon visit Egypt?
No, he didn't.

1 Did Simon visit Italy?
_____

2 Did it rain?
_____

3 Did Simon visit Pisa?
_____

4 Did Simon visit Rome?
_____

5 Did Simon like the food in Italy?
_____

6 Did Simon and Carol go waterskiing?
_____

7 Did Carol like waterskiing?
_____

8 Did Simon like waterskiing?
_____

9 Did Simon buy Carly a present?
_____

29.5 MATCH THE QUESTIONS WITH THE CORRECT ANSWERS

Why did you go there?	We took the bus.
① Who did you stay with?	On Wednesday evening.
② What did you visit while you were there?	At 11pm.
③ What time did you arrive at the airport?	Because I love Italian food.
④ How did you get there?	Some wonderful fish.
⑤ When did you come back?	With Marco's cousins.
⑥ What did you eat there?	The Tower of Pisa.

29.6 READ THE POSTCARD AND ANSWER THE QUESTIONS

Dear Kim,
Greetings from London. We arrived on Wednesday, and then we went straight to the London Eye. It's amazing! On Thursday we visited the Tower of London. I bought a T-shirt in the shop there. Then yesterday we took a boat on the Thames and went to Greenwich. In the evening we had fish and chips.
Phil

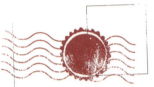

When did Phil arrive in London?	Wednesday ✓ Thursday ☐ Friday ☐
① When did he go to the Tower of London?	Wednesday ☐ Thursday ☐ Friday ☐
② What did Phil buy at the Tower of London?	Tie ☐ A T-shirt ☐ A poster ☐
③ How did Phil travel to Greenwich?	By taxi ☐ By bus ☐ By boat ☐
④ What did Phil eat in Greenwich?	A burger ☐ Pizza ☐ Fish and chips ☐

29.7 REWRITE THE SENTENCES, PUTTING THE WORDS IN THE CORRECT ORDER

did Why you Brazil? go to

Why did you go to Brazil?

① you When did Hong Kong? visit

_____

② travel with? Who you did

_____

③ you did evening? What eat in the

_____

④ buy did What there? you

_____

⑤ How to get the airport? you did

_____

⑥ visit What did Rome? in you

_____

⑦ do What you did Las Vegas? in

_____

29.8 SAY THE QUESTIONS OUT LOUD, FILLING IN THE GAPS

What _____*did you do*_____ on vacation?

We went walking in the mountains.

① Where _____ on vacation?

We went to France.

② When _____ at the hotel?

At about 9pm.

③ Who _____ on vacation with?

I went with my sister.

④ How _____ to the airport?

We took a taxi.

⑤ Why _____ to Sardinia?

Because it's a beautiful island.

⑥ What _____ at the restaurant?

We had fish and chips.

⑦ What _____ in Mallorca?

We went to some beautiful beaches.

30 Applying for a job

If you want to find a job, you need to understand the English words and phrases used in advertisements and on recruitment websites.

⚙ **New language** Interview responses
Aa Vocabulary Job words and phrases
🧩 **New skill** Dealing with job applications

30.1 READ THE JOB ADVERTISEMENTS AND ANSWER THE QUESTIONS

JOBS

WANTED
Vet at Whiskers Animal Centre, full time. Do you have a passion for animals? We need a vet to join our team. Two years' experience needed. £30,000 a year.

WANTED
Receptionist at Brown Law Firm, part-time. Are you friendly and outgoing? Do you work well in a team? We need a receptionist to work on Fridays and Saturdays (8am to 4pm), £10 an hour.

WANTED
Waiter at Alfredo's Pizzeria, evenings. We're looking for a hardworking waiter. Experience needed. Tuesday to Saturday (5pm to 11:30pm).

The job at Whiskers Animal Center is part time.
True ☐   False ☑

1 No experience is needed for the job as a vet.
True ☐   False ☐

2 The job at Brown Law Firm is on Thursdays.
True ☐   False ☐

3 The job at Brown Law Firm is part-time.
True ☐   False ☐

4 The waiter job is at lunchtimes.
True ☐   False ☐

5 You need some experience for the waiter job.
True ☐   False ☐

30.2 LISTEN TO THE AUDIO, THEN NUMBER THE QUESTIONS IN THE ORDER THAT YOU HEAR THEM

These are some questions that you may be asked at a job interview.

A Why did you study English in college? ☐
B Why would you like this job? ☐
C What experience do you have? ☐ 1
D What do you like doing in your free time? ☐

E When can you start work? ☐
F Did you enjoy your time at chef school? ☐
G Why did you leave your last job? ☐
H Do you like working with people? ☐

30.3 READ GARY'S COVER LETTER AND FILL IN THE GAPS IN THE DESCRIPTION OF HIS CAREER

Gary _would like_ to apply for a job at LinguaPlus.

1 He _____ an English teacher for two years.

2 He _____ English in college.

3 While _____ a student, he worked in a bar.

4 He _____ working with others.

5 Gary _____ English at St. Mark's School.

6 He _____ at BKS Language Services.

7 He _____ adults English now.

8 He _____ soccer in his free time.

9 He also _____ walking in the mountains.

Dear Mrs. O'Hanlon,

I would like to apply for the position of English teacher at LinguaPlus language school. I have been an English teacher for two years.

I studied English at Southern College. While I was a student I worked at Marco's Bar. I really liked working with other people.

After university, I worked at St. Mark's School, where I taught English. I am now working at BKS Language Services, where I teach adults English.

In my free time I love playing soccer and walking in the mountains.

I look forward to hearing from you soon.

Gary Smith

30.4 SAY THE QUESTIONS OUT LOUD, FILLING IN THE GAPS

What _did you study_ (study) at Manchester University?

1 What _____ (do) at your last job at the restaurant?

2 When _____ (start) working for our college?

3 Why _____ (want) to work for our company?

4 Where _____ (see) yourself in five years' time?

5 _____ (like) working with other people?

6 Why _____ (leave) your last job as a receptionist?

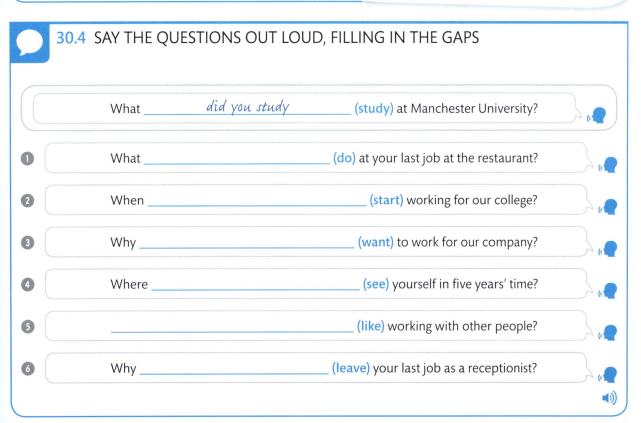

31 Types of questions

There are two kinds of questions: subject questions and object questions. You form them in different ways in order to ask about different things.

⚙ **New language** Subject and object questions
Aa Vocabulary Workplace words
🧩 **New skill** Asking different kinds of questions

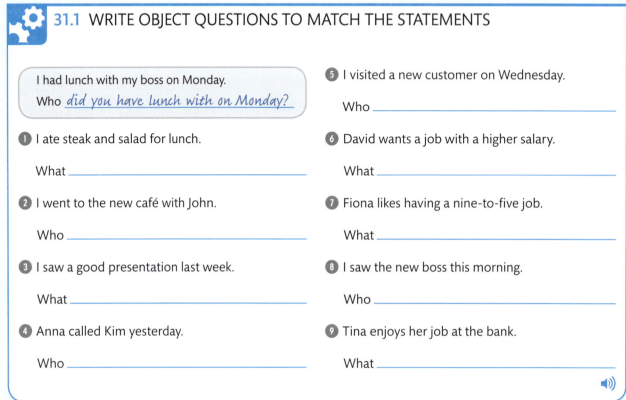

31.1 WRITE OBJECT QUESTIONS TO MATCH THE STATEMENTS

I had lunch with my boss on Monday.
Who _did you have lunch with on Monday?_

❶ I ate steak and salad for lunch.

What _____

❷ I went to the new café with John.

Who _____

❸ I saw a good presentation last week.

What _____

❹ Anna called Kim yesterday.

Who _____

❺ I visited a new customer on Wednesday.

Who _____

❻ David wants a job with a higher salary.

What _____

❼ Fiona likes having a nine-to-five job.

What _____

❽ I saw the new boss this morning.

Who _____

❾ Tina enjoys her job at the bank.

What _____

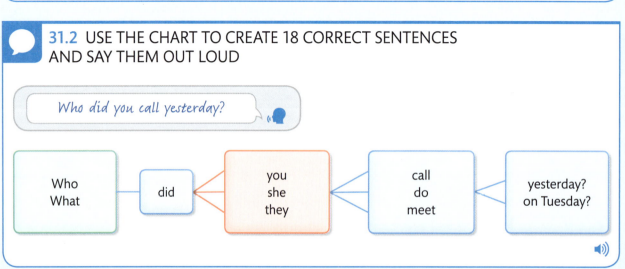

31.2 USE THE CHART TO CREATE 18 CORRECT SENTENCES AND SAY THEM OUT LOUD

Who did you call yesterday?

| Who / What | did | you / she / they | call / do / meet | yesterday? / on Tuesday? |

31.3 REWRITE THE SENTENCES, PUTTING THE WORDS IN THE CORRECT ORDER

this | sent | last | week? | Who | letter

Who sent this letter last week?

1 yesterday? | bank | called | the | Who

_____

2 new | did | order? | the | What | customer

_____

3 raise? | the | gave | a | Who | staff

_____

4 the | did | at | Who | meeting? | see | you

_____

5 the | does | want? | manager | What

_____

6 salary? | wants | Who | higher | a

_____

7 the | you? | say | What | boss | to | did

_____

8 call | on | Who | you | Monday? | did

_____

9 meeting | start? | What | time | the | did

_____

31.4 REWRITE THE STATEMENTS AS SUBJECT QUESTIONS

His old manager paid him a higher salary.
Who *paid him a higher salary?*

1 Stella emailed the prices to the customer.
Who _____

2 Harry started a full-time job last month.
Who _____

3 Paul doesn't want a nine-to-five job.
Who _____

4 The manager gave a presentation about sales.
Who _____

5 Alex and Joe had a good meeting yesterday.
Who _____

6 John didn't come to the meeting this morning.
Who _____

7 Dan started work at 7am today.
Who _____

8 Maria won the prize for Manager of the Month.
Who _____

9 The new office is big enough for the staff.
What _____

10 Jack wants to work for your company.
Who _____

11 The office party was great this year.
What _____

12 The new customer wants a discount.
Who _____

31.5 FILL IN THE GAPS USING "WHO" OR "WHAT" TO COMPLETE THE QUESTIONS

_____Who_____ bought a new laptop?

1 _____ asked for a higher salary?

2 _____ did Phil give the staff?

3 _____ gave a presentation?

4 _____ did she cook today?

5 _____ kind of job do you have?

6 _____ started a new job today?

7 _____ did you buy for Carla?

8 _____ didn't hit his sales targets?

9 _____ does she work for?

10 _____ sent the boss an email?

11 _____ did they say yesterday?

12 _____ did she meet on Tuesday?

13 _____ did you tell Amanda?

14 _____ asked for a discount?

15 _____ spoke to the customer?

16 _____ kind of music do you like?

17 _____ has a part-time job?

18 _____ gave the staff a day off?

19 _____ did Dan send the boss?

31.6 LISTEN TO THE AUDIO AND ANSWER THE QUESTIONS

Carlos is telling Sarah about a meeting he had in a restaurant.

When did Carlos go to the new restaurant?
Wednesday ☐ Friday ✓ Thursday ☐

1 Who did Carlos have lunch with last week?
his boss ☐ his brother ☐ his friend ☐

2 Did they like the food?
yes ☐ no ☐ they didn't order any ☐

3 Who had the special pizza?
Carlos ☐ his boss ☐ both of them ☐

4 Where is Carlos' new customer from?
Australia ☐ Canada ☐ the US ☐

5 What does his new customer's company make?
IT hardware ☐ IT software ☐ both ☐

6 Who does Carlos' new customer want to sell to?
the US ☐ Canada ☐ the UK ☐

7 How much is the bonus Carlos is getting?
£100 ☐ £300 ☐ £500 ☐

8 What other reward might Carlos get?
a promotion ☐ a holiday ☐ a raise ☐

9 Who does Sarah want to take to the restaurant?
Carlos ☐ Carlos' boss ☐ her boss ☐

31.7 MARK THE QUESTIONS THAT ARE CORRECT

Who did give you the present? ☐
Who gave you the present? ☑

① Who wrote to the customers? ☐
Who did write to the customers? ☐

② Who met their sales targets this month? ☐
Who meet their sales targets this month? ☐

③ What asked the customer for? ☐
What did the customer ask for? ☐

④ Who did give a presentation? ☐
Who gave a presentation? ☐

⑤ What did the manager give the staff? ☐
What gave the manager the staff? ☐

⑥ Who called the new customers? ☐
Who did call the new customers? ☐

⑦ What ordered the new customer? ☐
What did the new customer order? ☐

⑧ What job did Sandra start last week? ☐
What job started Sandra last week? ☐

⑨ What time started the meeting? ☐
What time did the meeting start? ☐

⑩ Who did take notes at the meeting? ☐
Who took notes at the meeting? ☐

⑪ What did the area manager want? ☐
What wanted the area manager? ☐

⑫ Who wants a higher salary? ☐
Who does want a higher salary? ☐

⑬ What said the boss to you yesterday? ☐
What did the boss say to you yesterday? ☐

⑭ Who did call on Monday? ☐
Who called you on Monday? ☐

⑮ Who gave you the notes from the meeting? ☐
Who give you the notes from the meeting? ☐

⑯ What kind of job does Karen have? ☐
What kind of job has Karen? ☐

⑰ Who did you see at the meeting? ☐
Who did you saw at the meeting? ☐

◀))

31.8 USE THE CHART TO CREATE SIX CORRECT SENTENCES AND SAY THEM OUT LOUD

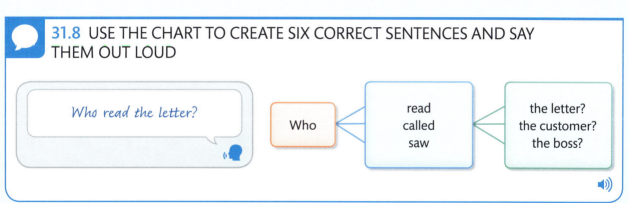

Who read the letter?

Who	read	the letter?
	called	the customer?
	saw	the boss?

◀))

32 Someone, anyone, everyone

Use indefinite pronouns such as "anyone," "someone," and "everyone," to refer to a person or a group of people without explaining who they are.

⚙ **New language** Indefinite pronouns
Aa **Vocabulary** Office words
🧩 **New skill** Talking about people in general

32.1 CROSS OUT THE INCORRECT WORD IN EACH SENTENCE

 I didn't see **anyone** / ~~someone~~ from school at the party on Saturday.

① There's **anyone** / **someone** at the door. Perhaps it's the new neighbor.

② My cousin wants **anyone** / **someone** to go on vacation with him to Argentina.

③ I need **anyone** / **someone** to help me with my homework. It's very difficult.

④ Does **anyone** / **someone** know John's phone number so I can give it to Sue?

⑤ I met **anyone** / **someone** interesting on vacation and we went to the beach together.

⑥ There's **anyone** / **someone** in the museum who you can ask for directions.

⑦ Is **anyone** / **someone** going to see the movie tonight with Rachel and Monica?

⑧ **Anyone** / **Someone** left an umbrella in the office on Monday.

⑨ I need **anyone** / **someone** to go to the party with me tonight.

⑩ Does **anyone** / **someone** want to go for coffee later in the café?

⑪ **Anyone** / **Someone** knocked on the door this morning when I was in the kitchen.

32.2 LISTEN TO THE AUDIO AND ANSWER THE QUESTIONS

Who went to the dance?
no one ☐ **everyone** ☐ **someone** ☑

1 Who wants some ice cream?
no one ☐ **everyone** ☐ **someone** ☐

2 Who saw the movie last night?
no one ☐ **everyone** ☐ **someone** ☐

3 Who is going abroad in the summer?
no one ☐ **everyone** ☐ **someone** ☐

4 Who wants to go to lunch with Sharon?
no one ☐ **everyone** ☐ **someone** ☐

5 Who likes the new boss?
no one ☐ **everyone** ☐ **someone** ☐

6 Who wants to go to a restaurant after work?
no one ☐ **everyone** ☐ **someone** ☐

7 Who will lend Kate a pencil?
no one ☐ **everyone** ☐ **someone** ☐

8 Who is going to the meeting later?
no one ☐ **everyone** ☐ **someone** ☐

32.3 REWRITE THE SENTENCES, CORRECTING THE ERRORS

Everybody **hate** our new office.
Everybody hates our new office.

1 I didn't give **nobody** your phone number.
_____

2 Is **somebody** coming for lunch with me?
_____

3 Nobody **like** my new green shirt.
_____

4 No one **are** coming to the movies tonight.
_____

5 **Anybody** remembered Ben's birthday. Poor Ben!
_____

6 Everyone **are** coming to my party tonight.
_____

7 Does **somebody** need help with the exercise?
_____

32.4 USE THE CHART TO CREATE NINE CORRECT SENTENCES AND SAY THEM OUT LOUD

Everybody went to the restaurant last night.

| Everybody Someone Nobody | went to asked wants | the restaurant last night. about the new job. to go to a party with me tonight. |

33 Making conversation

Short questions are a way of showing interest when you are talking with someone. Use them to keep the conversation going.

⚙ **New language** Short questions
Aa **Vocabulary** Question words
🧩 **New skill** Asking short questions

⚙ **33.1 MARK THE CORRECT SHORT QUESTION FOR EACH STATEMENT**

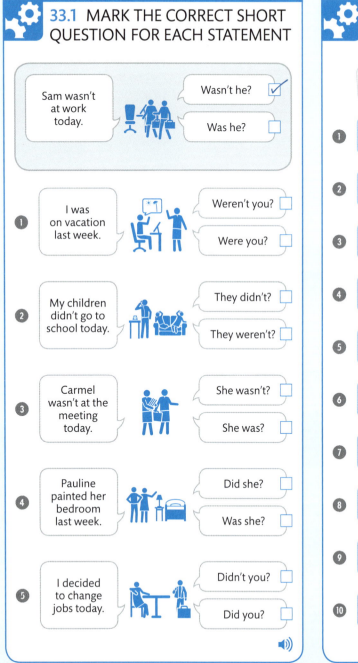

Sam wasn't at work today.
Wasn't he? ✓
Was he?

1 I was on vacation last week.
Weren't you?
Were you?

2 My children didn't go to school today.
They didn't?
They weren't?

3 Carmel wasn't at the meeting today.
She wasn't?
She was?

4 Pauline painted her bedroom last week.
Did she?
Was she?

5 I decided to change jobs today.
Didn't you?
Did you?

⚙ **33.2 MATCH THE STATEMENTS TO THEIR SHORT QUESTIONS**

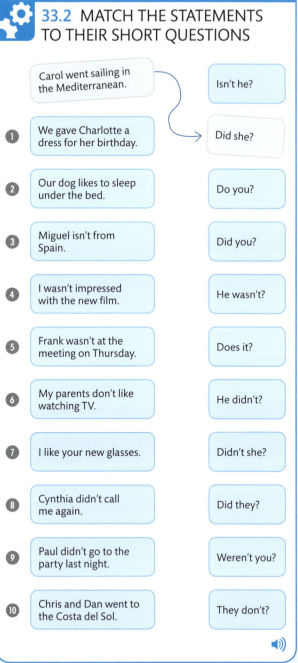

Carol went sailing in the Mediterranean.
Isn't he?

1 We gave Charlotte a dress for her birthday.
Did she?

2 Our dog likes to sleep under the bed.
Do you?

3 Miguel isn't from Spain.
Did you?

4 I wasn't impressed with the new film.
He wasn't?

5 Frank wasn't at the meeting on Thursday.
Does it?

6 My parents don't like watching TV.
He didn't?

7 I like your new glasses.
Didn't she?

8 Cynthia didn't call me again.
Did they?

9 Paul didn't go to the party last night.
Weren't you?

10 Chris and Dan went to the Costa del Sol.
They don't?

33.3 COMPLETE THE SHORT QUESTIONS BASED ON THE STATEMENTS

I really want to see the new movie.

_____Do_____ you?

1 Maria likes listening to opera.

_____ she?

2 Phillip went to Greece on vacation.

He _____ ?

3 Greg comes from Australia.

_____ he?

4 I don't have a car.

You _____ ?

5 My children hate reading books.

They _____ ?

6 Shelly isn't at home right now.

_____ she?

7 Kim wasn't at the party last night.

_____ she?

33.4 RESPOND TO THE AUDIO, SPEAKING OUT LOUD

Mario really likes rock.

_____Does_____ he?

1 I bought a great new book today.

_____ you?

2 Pete was very tired last week.

He _____ ?

3 We didn't visit the British Museum.

_____ you?

4 Ben and Katy sold their house.

_____ they?

5 It was really cold on our vacation.

_____ it?

6 I met my brother last night for a drink.

You _____ ?

7 Our cat absolutely loves fish.

It _____ ?

8 We bought a new car last week

_____ you?

9 Carl went to Las Vegas with his brother.

_____ he?

Aa 34.1 GOING OUT WRITE THE WORDS FROM THE PANEL UNDER THE CORRECT PICTURES

show

① _____

② _____

③ _____

④ _____

⑤ _____

⑦ _____

⑧ _____

⑨ _____

⑩ _____

⑪ _____

⑭ _____

⑮ _____

⑯ _____

⑰ _____

⑱ _____

㉑ _____

㉒ _____

㉓ _____

㉔ _____

㉕ _____

 5 _____

 6 _____

 12 _____

 13 _____

 19 _____

 20 _____

 26 _____

 27 _____

art gallery   bar   go bowling

buy a ticket   fun fair   opera

~~show~~   go dancing

circus   musician   orchestra

meet friends   waitress

menu   night club   audience

restaurant   see a play

concert hall   applause   waiter

book club   concert

do karaoke   ballet   go to a party

band   go to the movies

35 Future arrangements

You can use the present continuous to talk about things that are happening now. You can also use it to talk about arrangements for the future.

⚙ **New language** Future with present continuous
Aa Vocabulary Excuses
✣ **New skill** Talking about future arrangements

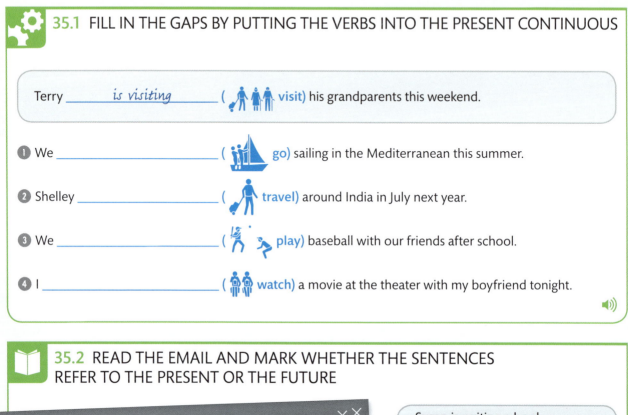

35.1 FILL IN THE GAPS BY PUTTING THE VERBS INTO THE PRESENT CONTINUOUS

Terry _____is visiting_____ (🚶‍👫 visit) his grandparents this weekend.

1 We _____ (⛵ go) sailing in the Mediterranean this summer.

2 Shelley _____ (🧳 travel) around India in July next year.

3 We _____ (⚾ play) baseball with our friends after school.

4 I _____ (🎬 watch) a movie at the theater with my boyfriend tonight.

🔊

35.2 READ THE EMAIL AND MARK WHETHER THE SENTENCES REFER TO THE PRESENT OR THE FUTURE

✉ ⌄ ✕

To: Carol

Subject: Plan for the week

Hi Carol,
Thanks for inviting me to dinner next week. I'm very busy at the moment, because I'm writing a book. But I'll tell you my plan for the week. On Monday and Tuesday, I'm playing tennis with Cathy. Cathy is living in London now. On Wednesday, I'm visiting Mike. Mike is working at the school on Grange Road. He really loves it there. On Thursday, I'm going swimming with Paula. It'll be great to see her.
Susan

↩ ↩↩ 📎 🗑

Susan is writing a book.
Present ✓   **Future** ☐

1 Susan is playing tennis with Cathy.
Present ☐   **Future** ☐

2 Cathy is living in London.
Present ☐   **Future** ☐

3 Mike is working at the school.
Present ☐   **Future** ☐

4 Susan is going swimming with Paula.
Present ☐   **Future** ☐

35.3 CROSS OUT THE INCORRECT WORD IN EACH SENTENCE

I'm graduating ~~on~~ / in 2016.

1 We're going to France on / in June.

2 I'm playing tennis on / in Wednesday.

3 My grandmother was born on / in 1944.

4 Christmas Day is on / in December 25.

5 I'm finishing work on / in 2025.

6 I bought a new car on / in Wednesday.

7 New Year's Day is on / in January 1.

8 Pete was born on / in 1990.

9 I saw my friend Clive on / in Saturday.

10 Derek starts his job on / in Tuesday.

11 Alexander's exam is on / in June 4.

12 We finish school on / in July.

13 I'm going to the theater on / in Friday evening.

◁))

35.4 RESPOND OUT LOUD TO THE AUDIO, PUTTING THE VERBS IN THE PANEL IN THE PRESENT CONTINUOUS

Would you like to go swimming this weekend?

Sorry, I can't. I _____*am visiting*_____ my grandmother.

1 Do you want to go to the movies tomorrow?

I'd love to, but I can't. I _____ for my exam.

2 Would you like to go to Franco's restaurant tonight?

That would be nice, but I _____ my girlfriend in town.

3 Would you like to play golf with me next week?

Oh, I'd love to, but I _____ on vacation to Spain.

4 Would you like to have lunch with us today?

I'd like to, but I can't. I _____ lunch with Sue today.

| have | study | go | meet | ~~visit~~ |

◁))

107

35.5 READ THE EMAIL AND ANSWER THE QUESTIONS

✉   ∨ ✕

To: Paul

Subject: Travel plans

Hi Paul,
Thanks for the invite! I'd love to come with you to
Italy, but I'm traveling to Greece in June. But I'm
coming to Paris in July, so hopefully we can meet
then. I have some news. My granddad is retiring. So,
we are having a party in August. All the family is
coming. I hope you'll be there. I'm having a really busy
week. I'm studying for my exams at the moment. I
have a big English exam on May 7. Then, on Tuesday,
I'm playing golf. It's a big competition, and I hope I'm
going to win. Aside from that, I'm going to the theater
with Emma tonight.
How are things with you?
Tony

↩ ↩↩   📎 🗑

Tony is traveling to Greece in July.
True ☐ **False** ✓

❶ Tony is coming to Paris in July.
True ☐ **False** ☐

❷ Tony's grandmother is retiring in August.
True ☐ **False** ☐

❸ Tony is studying for his English exam.
True ☐ **False** ☐

❹ Tony's exam is on May 8.
True ☐ **False** ☐

❺ Tony is playing tennis on Tuesday.
True ☐ **False** ☐

35.6 LISTEN TO THE AUDIO AND MATCH THE NAMES TO THE EXCUSES

Diane → I would love to, but I'm working that evening.

I'm sorry, but I'm going to the theater that evening.

❶ Jane

❷ Daniel — That sounds nice, but I'm going on vacation to Mexico.

❸ Lee — Sorry, I can't. I'm studying for my exams then.

❹ Bill — Sorry, I can't. I'm going to see a band.

❺ Sanjay — I'd like to, but I'm going to dinner with Carl that night.

❻ Carlo — Sorry, I can't. I'm having lunch with Irene.

❼ Rachel — I'd love to, but I'm meeting my sister that day.

❽ May — That sounds nice, but I'm going shopping with Tom.

❾ Sarah — I'd love to, but I'm playing soccer with my colleagues.

35.7 READ THE DIARY, THEN ANSWER THE QUESTIONS, SPEAKING OUT LOUD

September

MONDAY 5	Go swimming
TUESDAY 6	Go to the movies
WEDNESDAY 7	Visit old friends from school
THURSDAY 8	Study for the math exam
FRIDAY 9	Go to Sam's party
SATURDAY 10	Visit my grandparents
SUNDAY 11	Go ice skating with Victoria
MONDAY 12	Shop for groceries

Would you like to come to dinner on Tuesday?

I would love to, but _I am going to the movies_ .

4 Would you like to play soccer on Friday?

That would be fun, but _____ _____ .

1 Do you want to play soccer on Sunday?

That'd be fun, but _____ _____ .

5 Do you want to go to a party on Saturday?

Sorry I can't. _____ _____ .

2 Would you like to go to a café on Monday?

I'd like to, but _____ _____ .

6 Would you like to go ice skating on Thursday?

That sounds nice, but _____ _____ .

3 Would you like to go running on Wednesday?

That sounds nice, but _____ _____ .

7 Do you want to go out for lunch next Monday?

I can't. _____ _____ .

36 Plans and intentions

You can use "going to" to talk about what you want to do in the future. Use it also to talk about specific plans, such as when and where you're going to do something.

⚙ **New language** Future tense
Aa Vocabulary Time words and phrases
🧩 **New skill** Talking about your plans

 36.1 READ THE EMAIL AND ANSWER THE QUESTIONS

Phil is going to have a quiet summer.	**True** ☐	**False** ☑

1 Phil is going to visit the Azores.   **True** ☐   **False** ☐

2 He is going to start a job in a bar.   **True** ☐   **False** ☐

3 Phil is going to a music festival.   **True** ☐   **False** ☐

4 It's going to be a jazz festival.   **True** ☐   **False** ☐

5 In August, Phil's going to Norway.   **True** ☐   **False** ☐

6 Julia's going to go, too.   **True** ☐   **False** ☐

✉

To: Jake

Subject: My summer plans

Hi Jake,
This summer is going to be really busy. I've got a lot of plans! In June I'm going on vacation. I'm going with Julia to the Azores. I can't wait! In July I'm going to start a job at a local café. It's only a few hours, but I want to save some money. Then later in July, I'm going to a music festival. A lot of my favorite heavy metal groups are going to play. In August I'm going to Scotland. Julia's not going to come because she has a new job.
Hope you have a good summer,
Phil

⚙ **36.2 CROSS OUT THE INCORRECT WORDS IN EACH SENTENCE**

I ~~is~~ / ~~are~~ / am going start a new language course.

1 Angela **is** / are / am going to clean her bedroom.

2 Will **is** / are / am not going to buy a new car.

3 They **is** / are / am going to stay in a hotel.

4 Mary and George **is** / are / am going to visit Egypt.

5 Shane **is** / are / am going to study IT in college.

6 You **is** / are / am going to visit your grandmother.

7 Liv **is** / are / am going to finish her work later.

8 Aziz **is** / are / am going to travel to Rome this fall.

9 They **is** / are / am not going to play soccer today.

10 I **is** / are / am going to cook steak tonight.

11 We **is** / are / am going to eat pizza for dinner.

12 Murat **is** / are / am going to listen to the radio.

13 I **is** / are / am not going to eat frogs' legs again.

🔊

36.3 REWRITE THE SENTENCES, PUTTING THE WORDS IN THE CORRECT ORDER

is | to | Karen | going | her | house. | paint

Karen is going to paint her house.

1 to | pizza | Tim | eat | tonight. | is | going

_____

2 not | is | drive | to | Ann | to | going | Utah.

_____

3 Boston | going | are | this | to | fall. | We | visit

_____

4 going | Fred | is | to | German. | study | not

_____

5 buy | are | going | They | to | a | puppy.

_____

6 I | to | this | am | travel | going | summer.

_____

7 soccer. | play | are | going | to | We

_____

8 going | I'm | start | to | an | English | course.

_____

9 is | to | her | clean | going | room. | Angela

_____

10 going | I | to | at | study | the | library. | am

_____

11 their | to | going | They | are | sell | house.

_____

36.4 FILL IN THE GAPS USING THE FUTURE TENSE WITH "GOING TO"

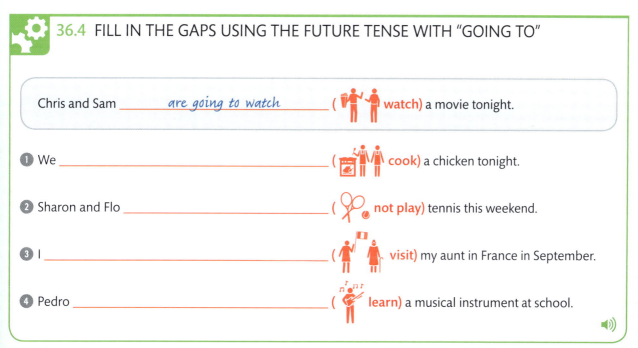

Chris and Sam _____*are going to watch*_____ (watch) a movie tonight.

1 We _____ (cook) a chicken tonight.

2 Sharon and Flo _____ (not play) tennis this weekend.

3 I _____ (visit) my aunt in France in September.

4 Pedro _____ (learn) a musical instrument at school.

Aa 36.5 MATCH THE PICTURES WITH THE DESCRIPTIONS

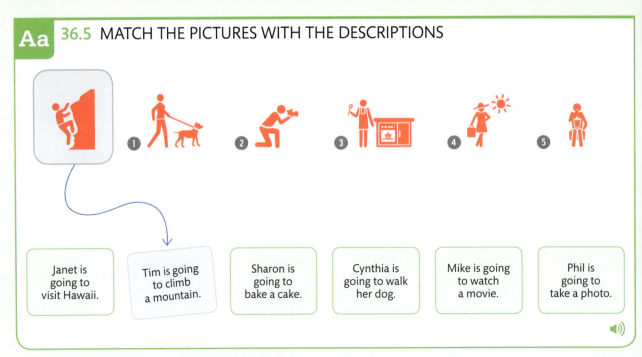

Janet is going to visit Hawaii.

Tim is going to climb a mountain.

Sharon is going to bake a cake.

Cynthia is going to walk her dog.

Mike is going to watch a movie.

Phil is going to take a photo.

36.6 SAY THE SENTENCES OUT LOUD, FILLING IN THE GAPS

You ___are going to watch___ (watch) a movie this evening.

5 Patrick _____ (not drive) to work today.

1 I _____ (visit) Berlin next week.

6 Angus _____ (live) in Edinburgh.

2 Rachel _____ (paint) her kitchen on the weekend.

7 We _____ (buy) a new house.

3 My sister _____ (study) French in college.

8 Samantha _____ (watch) a movie tonight.

4 Stuart and Colin _____ (climb) that mountain.

9 Helen _____ (start) her new job next week.

112

36.7 MATCH THE BEGINNINGS OF THE SENTENCES TO THE CORRECT ENDINGS

Tom is going to save — enough money by Christmas.

1 Jessica is not going to study

2 We are going to paint

3 Jenny is going to go

4 Theo is going to wear a suit

5 My uncle is not going to eat

6 Olivia is going to ride

7 I am going to bake

a cake for Christmas.

for his job interview.

a hamburger for lunch.

enough money by Christmas.

the kitchen a different color.

her horse this weekend.

physics in college.

on vacation in the Bahamas.

 36.8 LISTEN TO THE AUDIO AND NUMBER THE PICTURES IN THE ORDER THEY ARE DESCRIBED

37 What's going to happen

Use the future with "going to" to make a prediction about the future when there is evidence in the present moment to back up that prediction.

⚙ **New language** The future with "going to"

Aa Vocabulary Prediction verbs

🧩 **New skill** Predicting future events

 37.1 LOOK AT THE PICTURES, THEN FILL IN THE GAPS USING THE VERBS IN THE PANEL

He's going to _____sing_____ a song.

1 The boy is going to _____ the wall.

2 It looks like it's going to _____ soon.

3 It's 8:29pm. We're going to _____ the train.

4 Oh dear! I think they're going to _____.

5 I think she's going to _____ that coat.

| fall off | crash | buy | rain | miss | ~~sing~~ |

Jenny has finished all her final exams. She are going to leave school soon.
Jenny has finished all her final exams. She is going to leave school soon.

❶ Oh no, it's started to rain cats and dogs. We going to get wet!

_____

❷ That girl has been teasing the dog all day. I think it is going bite her.

_____

❸ Hurry up! The train leaves in five minutes and you is going to miss it.

_____

❹ That's Claire's purse. She's going leave for college in a minute.

_____

❺ It looks like he going to win this race. He's a long way in front.

_____

❻ The team captain has a microphone. Do you think he's going sing the national anthem?

_____

❼ The weather forecast says it are not going to rain at all next week.

_____

❽ This traffic jam is enormous. I is going to be late for work again.

_____

❾ That dog is trying to open your shopping bag. I think he's go to steal your food.

_____

❿ Raymond are going to study science in college.

_____

⓫ Shelley not going to win the competition. The other players are all too good.

_____

⓬ They're not very good at skating. It looks like they is going to fall over.

_____

◀))

37.3 REWRITE THE SENTENCES, PUTTING THE WORDS IN THE CORRECT ORDER

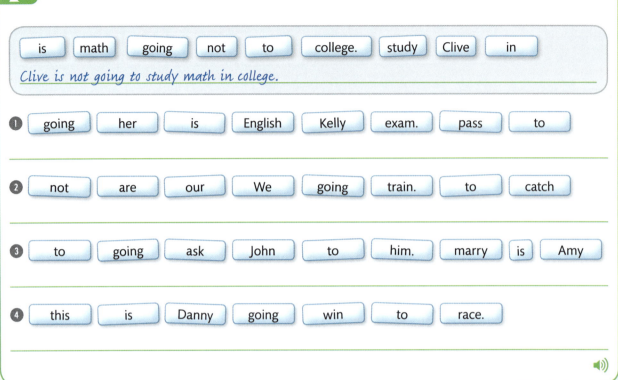

| is | math | going | not | to | college. | study | Clive | in |

Clive is not going to study math in college.

❶ | going | her | is | English | Kelly | exam. | pass | to |

_____

❷ | not | are | our | We | going | train. | to | catch |

_____

❸ | to | going | ask | John | to | him. | marry | is | Amy |

_____

❹ | this | is | Danny | going | win | to | race. |

_____

🔊

Aa 37.4 MATCH THE BEGINNINGS OF THE SENTENCES TO THE CORRECT ENDINGS

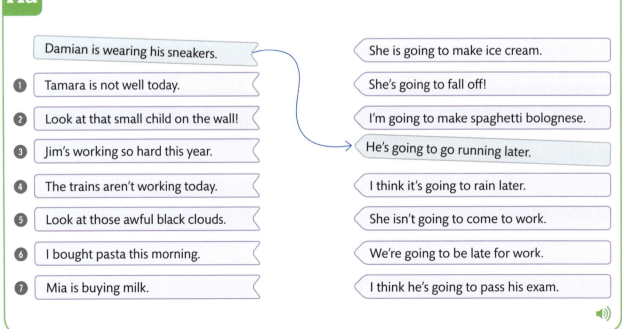

Damian is wearing his sneakers.

She is going to make ice cream.

❶ Tamara is not well today.

She's going to fall off!

❷ Look at that small child on the wall!

I'm going to make spaghetti bolognese.

❸ Jim's working so hard this year.

He's going to go running later.

❹ The trains aren't working today.

I think it's going to rain later.

❺ Look at those awful black clouds.

She isn't going to come to work.

❻ I bought pasta this morning.

We're going to be late for work.

❼ Mia is buying milk.

I think he's going to pass his exam.

🔊

37.5 FILL IN THE GAPS BY PUTTING THE VERBS IN THE FUTURE WITH "GOING TO"

Charmaine _____*is going to send*_____ (send) a letter.

1. Sharon _____ (eat) a piece of cake.

2. Take an umbrella. It _____ (rain) later.

3. The children _____ (enjoy) the movie tonight.

4. My husband _____ (be) late for work.

5. Mrs. O'Connell _____ (play) the piano in a minute.

6. Be careful! You _____ (drop) the vase.

7. Bill and Claire _____ (bake) a birthday cake for Paul.

 37.6 USE THE CHART TO CREATE 18 CORRECT SENTENCES AND SAY THEM OUT LOUD

I am going to be late for work.

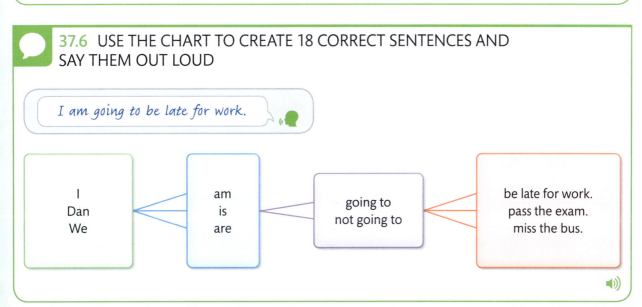

| I
Dan
We | am
is
are | going to
not going to | be late for work.
pass the exam.
miss the bus. |

Aa 38.1 ANIMALS WRITE THE WORDS FROM THE PANEL UNDER THE CORRECT PICTURES

eagle

1 _____

2 _____

3 _____

4 _____

8 _____

9 _____

10 _____

11 _____

12 _____

16 _____

17 _____

18 _____

19 _____

20 _____

24 _____

25 _____

26 _____

27 _____

28 _____

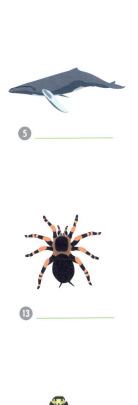

5 _____

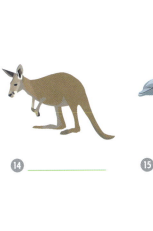

6 _____

7 _____

13 _____

14 _____

15 _____

21 _____

22 _____

23 _____

29 _____

30 _____

31 _____

lion   giraffe

rhino   bull

elephant   ~~eagle~~

bee   dolphin

butterfly   snake

lizard   fish

octopus   cow

buffalo   monkey

spider   crab

shark   tiger

bird   rat   insect

fly   turtle   bear

crocodile   camel

whale   mouse

kangaroo   frog

39 Making predictions

You can use the verb "will" to talk about future events in English. This form of the future tense has a slightly different meaning from futures using "going to."

⚙ **New language** The future with "will"
Aa **Vocabulary** Prediction words
🧩 **New skill** Saying what you think will happen

⚙ **39.1** FILL IN THE GAPS, PUTTING THE VERBS IN THE FUTURE WITH "WILL"

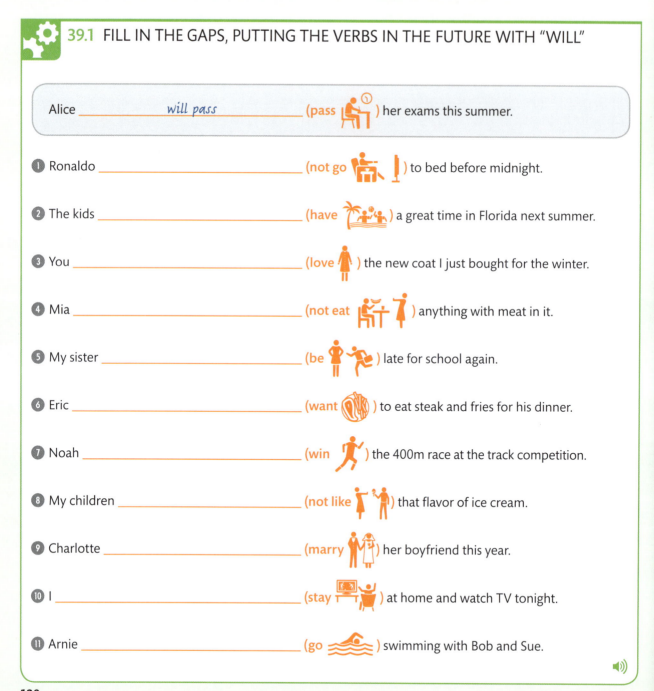

Alice _____ *will pass* _____ (pass) her exams this summer.

1 Ronaldo _____ (not go) to bed before midnight.

2 The kids _____ (have) a great time in Florida next summer.

3 You _____ (love) the new coat I just bought for the winter.

4 Mia _____ (not eat) anything with meat in it.

5 My sister _____ (be) late for school again.

6 Eric _____ (want) to eat steak and fries for his dinner.

7 Noah _____ (win) the 400m race at the track competition.

8 My children _____ (not like) that flavor of ice cream.

9 Charlotte _____ (marry) her boyfriend this year.

10 I _____ (stay) at home and watch TV tonight.

11 Arnie _____ (go) swimming with Bob and Sue.

39.2 REWRITE THE SENTENCES USING THE SHORT FORMS OF "WILL" AND "WILL NOT"

We will go to the shops.	=	*We'll go to the shops.*

1 Chris will not go on vacation this year. = _____

2 I will write you a postcard from Ibiza. = _____

3 They will visit their grandmother next week. = _____

4 Ethan will not go to summer camp this year. = _____

5 Isla will not reply to my messages. = _____

6 We will visit you when we are in San Diego. = _____

7 I will not be at the party this evening. = _____

8 Eleanor will not make dinner for us tonight. = _____

9 I will take the children to the movie theater tonight. = _____

10 Fred will not be at the party tomorrow. = _____

🔊

39.3 REWRITE THE HIGHLIGHTED PHRASES USING A PRONOUN AND THE CONTRACTED FORM OF THE VERB

She'll bring some salad.

1 _____

2 _____

3 _____

4 _____

5 _____

Hi Peter,

The picnic on Saturday is going to be fantastic. I can't wait. Is there anything you'd like me to bring? Chloe will bring some salad. She always makes one for us. David will bring some chicken and Sarah will make some sandwiches. I think Martha will get some juice. Hopefully Sharon and Andrew will make a cake. I just hope the weather will be nice and sunny! I can bring some salami and some cheese if you like.

See you Saturday,

Doug

39.4 REWRITE THE SENTENCES WITH "I THINK" OR "I DON'T THINK"

> It won't rain this afternoon.
> *I don't think it will rain this afternoon.*

1 I'll visit Rome next year.

_____

2 Bob won't be at the party.

_____

3 We'll go to a restaurant tonight.

_____

4 My brother will visit us this year.

_____

5 The kids won't go to school tomorrow.

_____

6 It won't be sunny tomorrow.

_____

7 We'll win the lottery this week.

_____

8 Simone will want to go to the theater.

_____

9 It won't snow this winter.

_____

39.5 CROSS OUT THE INCORRECT WORDS IN EACH SENTENCE

> I think you ~~are going to~~ / will really enjoy this book.

TIP
Use "will" for predictions without evidence and "going to" for predictions with evidence.

1 Look at those clouds. It **is going to** / will rain.

2 You **isn't going to** / won't like this movie.

3 There's so much traffic! We **are going to** / will be late.

4 Bob never does his homework. He **is going to** / will fail the exam.

5 **Will he** / **Are he going to** come to the party tomorrow?

6 Jenny practices the guitar every day. She **is going to** / will be a great musician.

7 Bob looks tired. He **isn't going to** / won't finish the race.

8 I think Chloe **is going to** / will not win the competition. I love her voice.

9 Peter **is going to** / will fall asleep. He looks tired.

10 It **is going to be** / will be a delicious meal.

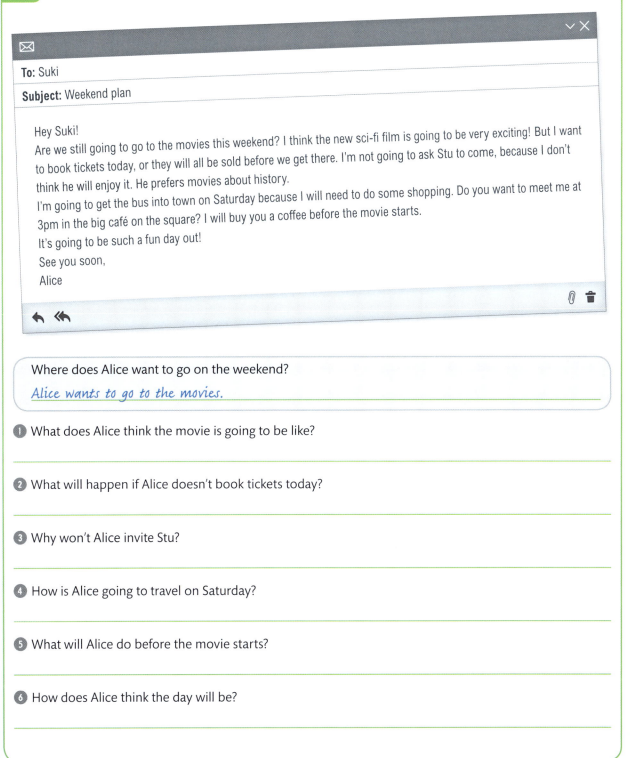

To: Suki

Subject: Weekend plan

Hey Suki!
Are we still going to go to the movies this weekend? I think the new sci-fi film is going to be very exciting! But I want to book tickets today, or they will all be sold before we get there. I'm not going to ask Stu to come, because I don't think he will enjoy it. He prefers movies about history.
I'm going to get the bus into town on Saturday because I will need to do some shopping. Do you want to meet me at 3pm in the big café on the square? I will buy you a coffee before the movie starts.
It's going to be such a fun day out!
See you soon,
Alice

Where does Alice want to go on the weekend?

Alice wants to go to the movies.

❶ What does Alice think the movie is going to be like?

_____

❷ What will happen if Alice doesn't book tickets today?

_____

❸ Why won't Alice invite Stu?

_____

❹ How is Alice going to travel on Saturday?

_____

❺ What will Alice do before the movie starts?

_____

❻ How does Alice think the day will be?

_____

40 Making quick decisions

You can use "will" to talk about the future in two ways: when you make a prediction without evidence, and when you make a quick decision to do something.

⚙ **New language** Quick decisions with "will"
Aa Vocabulary Decision words
New skill Talking about future actions

40.1 FILL IN THE GAPS BY PUTTING THE VERBS INTO THE FUTURE USING "WILL" AND "WON'T"

It's raining, so we ____*won't walk*____ (not walk). We ____*will go*____ (go) there by car.

❶ There's no milk, so I _____ (not have) tea. I _____ (have) black coffee.

❷ The 11:05 train is late, so we _____ (not get) that one. We _____ (take) the bus.

❸ I don't feel well. I _____ (not go) to work. I _____ (call) my boss and tell him.

❹ I left work late yesterday. I _____ (not stay) late today. I _____ (leave) at 5pm.

❺ I'm tired. I _____ (not make) dinner. I _____ (ask) my partner to make it.

❻ There are no buses and it's raining. I _____ (not walk) . I _____ (get) a taxi home.

❼ It is snowing. I _____ (not drive) to work. I _____ (get) the bus today.

❽ It's late. I _____ (not walk) the dog in the park. I _____ (walk) up the road instead.

❾ It's sunny. I _____ (not take) an umbrella. I _____ (wear) my sun hat.

❿ There's a lot of traffic. I _____ (not drive) . I _____ (walk) there.

⓫ I _____ (not take) my books back to the library. I _____ (do) it tomorrow.

40.2 LISTEN TO THE AUDIO AND MARK WHETHER THE SPEAKERS WILL OR WON'T DO THE ACTIVITIES

Will do ✓   Won't do ☐

❶ Will do ☐   Won't do ☐

❷ Will do ☐   Won't do ☐

❸ Will do ☐   Won't do ☐

❹ Will do ☐   Won't do ☐

❺ Will do ☐   Won't do ☐

40.3 MATCH THE BEGINNINGS OF THE SENTENCES TO THE CORRECT ENDINGS

There's too much traffic, so

❶ It's going to rain, so

❷ It's my sister's birthday today, so

❸ I forgot my sandwich, so

❹ I like those jeans, so

❺ It's dark, so

❻ It's a long train trip, so

❼ There's nothing to eat, so

I'll make her a cake.

I'll take a book with me.

I'll buy them.

I'll walk there.

I won't walk home through the park.

I'll take an umbrella with me.

I'll get a takeout pizza.

I'll buy one from the deli.

40.4 RESPOND OUT LOUD TO THE AUDIO, USING THE WORDS IN THE PANEL

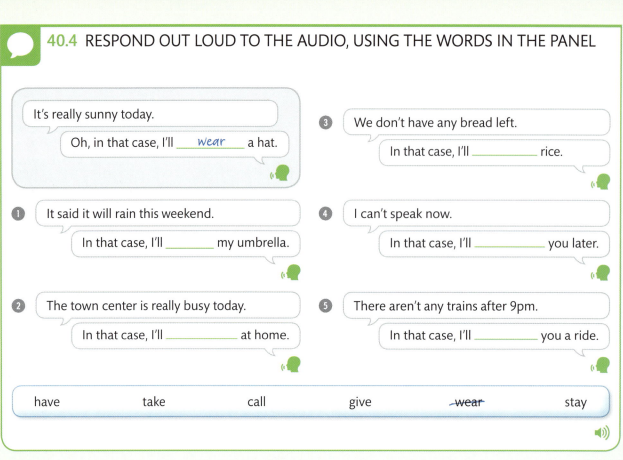

It's really sunny today.

Oh, in that case, I'll ___wear___ a hat.

① It said it will rain this weekend.

In that case, I'll _____ my umbrella.

② The town center is really busy today.

In that case, I'll _____ at home.

③ We don't have any bread left.

In that case, I'll _____ rice.

④ I can't speak now.

In that case, I'll _____ you later.

⑤ There aren't any trains after 9pm.

In that case, I'll _____ you a ride.

have   take   call   give   ~~wear~~   stay

40.5 REWRITE THE SENTENCES, PUTTING THE WORDS IN THE CORRECT ORDER

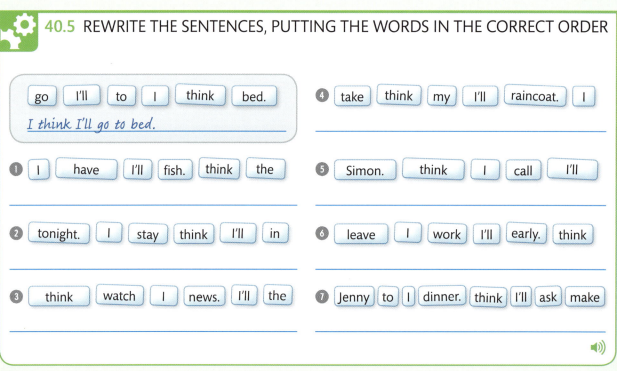

go   I'll   to   I   think   bed.

I think I'll go to bed.

① I   have   I'll   fish.   think   the

② tonight.   I   stay   think   I'll   in

③ think   watch   I   news.   I'll   the

④ take   think   my   I'll   raincoat.   I

⑤ Simon.   think   I   call   I'll

⑥ leave   I   work   I'll   early.   think

⑦ Jenny   to   I   dinner.   think   I'll   ask   make

126

40.6 READ THE GROUP CHAT AND ANSWER THE QUESTIONS

It's the English class party next Friday.
True ✓ False ☐

1 Two students will decorate with balloons.
True ☐ False ☐

2 John won't help Kate.
True ☐ False ☐

3 Everyone will make a banner with their names on it.
True ☐ False ☐

4 Harry will arrange the music for the party.
True ☐ False ☐

5 Josie's band will definitely play at the party.
True ☐ False ☐

6 Arthur will play in a band at the party.
True ☐ False ☐

7 Janet will make two cakes.
True ☐ False ☐

Student group chat

Mrs Jones: Can anyone help me with the English class party next Friday? There's lots to organize!

Kate: I'll decorate with balloons.

John: I'll help you, Kate. I think I'll make a banner with everyone's name on it.

Harry: I'll play the music. I'll make a party playlist from the class's favorite songs.

Josie: I play in a band. I think I'll ask them if they can play.

Arthur: I hope they can. I will definitely come if they do.

Janet: What about food? I'll make a chocolate cake and a lemon cake.

40.7 USE THE CHART TO CREATE 10 CORRECT SENTENCES AND SAY THEM OUT LOUD

I think he'll win the race.

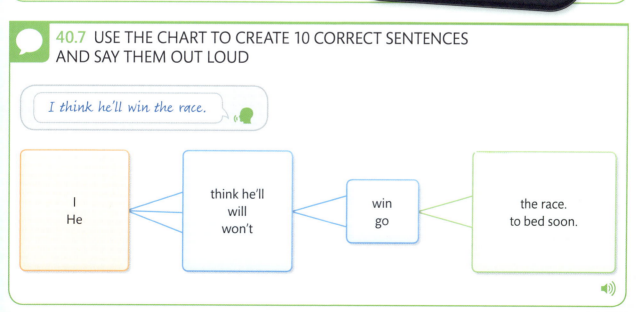

| I / He | think he'll / will / won't | win / go | the race. / to bed soon. |

41 Future possibilities

Use "might" to show you're not sure if you'll do something. It's a possibility and you don't want to say that you "will" or you "won't."

⚙ **New language** Using "might"
Aa Vocabulary Activities, food, and pastimes
New skill Talking about future possibilities

⚙ **41.1** REWRITE THE SENTENCES, PUTTING THE WORDS IN THE CORRECT ORDER

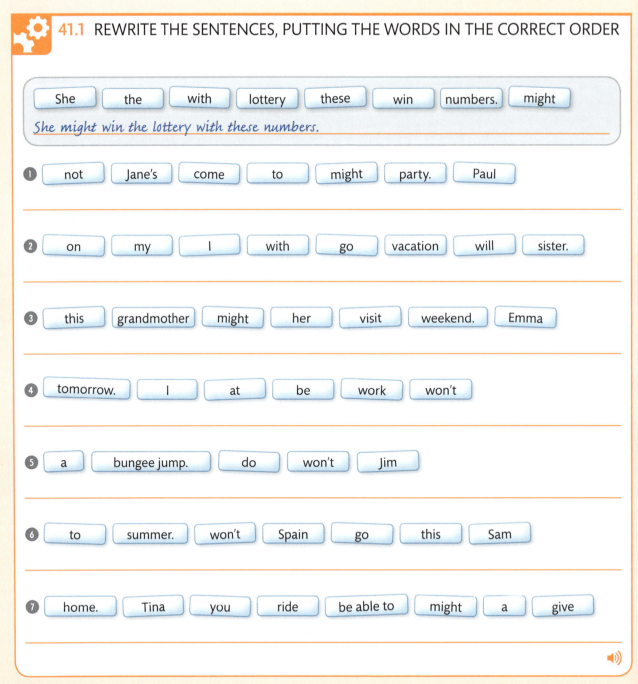

She | the | with | lottery | these | win | numbers. | might

She might win the lottery with these numbers.

1 not | Jane's | come | to | might | party. | Paul

2 on | my | I | with | go | vacation | will | sister.

3 this | grandmother | might | her | visit | weekend. | Emma

4 tomorrow. | I | at | be | work | won't

5 a | bungee jump. | do | won't | Jim

6 to | summer. | won't | Spain | go | this | Sam

7 home. | Tina | you | ride | be able to | might | a | give

41.2 FILL IN THE GAPS TO WRITE EACH SENTENCE IN THREE DIFFERENT WAYS

I **won't** buy a computer.	I *might buy a computer.*	I *will buy a computer.*

1 _____ I **might** go to the movies tonight. _____

2 We **won't** go to Dan's party. _____ _____

3 _____ _____ I **will** go to the bank at lunchtime.

4 _____ I **might** buy a newspaper. _____

5 You **won't** work late tonight. _____ _____

6 _____ _____ Karen **will** move next month.

41.3 REWRITE THE HIGHLIGHTED PHRASES, CORRECTING THE ERRORS

To: Eric

Subject: Travel plans

Hi Eric,

I'm planning where to travel next year. <mark>I might</mark> definitely need a break after all my hard work recently, but <mark>I won't</mark> need to book something quickly or <mark>it wills</mark> get too expensive. <mark>I will</mark> go too far away, as I don't like long flights. <mark>I won't</mark> be sick of the cold weather, so <mark>I mights</mark> go somewhere hot with nice beaches. <mark>I wont</mark> spend all my time on the beach, though. <mark>I won't</mark> do some hiking as well. <mark>I'might</mark> even try surfing. <mark>It won't</mark> be fantastic! <mark>I mighty</mark> want someone to come with me. <mark>Won't you</mark> be free in February? Let me know!

Darran

I will

1 _____

2 _____

3 _____

4 _____

5 _____

6 _____

7 _____

8 _____

9 _____

10 _____

11 _____

41.4 MATCH THE QUESTIONS AND ANSWERS

When will you clean your room? — I might do it this afternoon.

I think Sean will give me a ride.

I don't know. I'm pretty tired.

1. Will you buy a new computer?
2. Where will you meet Anna?
3. Will you go to John's party?
4. How will you get to the station?
5. What will you do this afternoon?
6. When will you get your exam results?
7. Who will you see at the party?
8. Will you make dinner tonight?
9. Where will you go on vacation this year?
10. What will you buy at the mall?

I'm not sure. Perhaps next Monday.

I don't know. I might buy some new shoes.

I'll meet her at the train station.

I'm not sure. I think I'll go to France.

I don't know, they're very expensive.

I don't know. I might see Katie.

I don't know. I think Diana will make it.

I don't know. I might watch a movie.

41.5 LISTEN TO THE AUDIO AND ANSWER THE QUESTIONS

Will John go to work today?
- Yes, he will. ☐
- He might. ✔
- No, he won't. ☐

1. Will Sally make dinner today?
- Yes, she will. ☐
- She might. ☐
- No, she won't. ☐

2. Will Nick go to the beach?
- Yes, he will. ☐
- He might. ☐
- No, he won't. ☐

3. Will Sara go to the movies this evening?
- Yes, she will. ☐
- She might. ☐
- No, she won't. ☐

4. Will Jim wash his car?
- Yes, he will. ☐
- He might. ☐
- No, he won't. ☐

5. Will Fiona go for a run this afternoon?
- Yes, she will. ☐
- She might. ☐
- No, she won't. ☐

41.6 LOOK AT THE CHART AND SAY OUT LOUD WHAT EACH PERSON "WILL", "MIGHT", AND "WON'T" DO

	WILL	MIGHT	WON'T
Sue			
❶ Adam			
❷ Leanne			
❸ Peter			
❹ Carla			
❺ Ken			

Sue will go bungee jumping.
She might read a book.
Sue won't go to the beach.

_____ ride a bike.
_____ watch a film.
_____ cook dinner.

_____ go running.
_____ play tennis.
_____ go to bed early.

_____ drive his car.
_____ walk home.
_____ ride a motorcycle.

_____ go to the hairdresser.
_____ go to the supermarket.
_____ go swimming.

_____ have coffee.
_____ read a newspaper.
_____ eat a burger.

42 Giving advice

If someone has a problem, one of the ways that you can give advice is by using the modal verb "should."

 New language "Should"

Aa Vocabulary Advice

 New skill Giving advice

Aa 42.1 LOOK AT THE PICTURES AND CROSS OUT THE INCORRECT WORD IN EACH SENTENCE

 Peter looks very stressed. He **should** / ~~shouldn't~~ take a week off work.

① It's dark and cold outside. You **should** / **shouldn't** walk home.

② Tim's driving later. He **should** / **shouldn't** drink that wine.

③ Clara is very tired. She **should** / **shouldn't** go to bed early tonight.

④ It's very cold here. You **should** / **shouldn't** wear a sweater.

⑤ Flora feels ill. She **should** / **shouldn't** go to the doctor tomorrow.

42.2 REWRITE THE SENTENCES, CORRECTING THE ERRORS

Patti should to work harder at school.
Patti should work harder at school.

① Carla shoulds take time off this year.

_____

② Casey shouldn't to buy herself a dog.

_____

③ Kevin should saves some money for his vacation.

_____

④ Rahul should to visit his mother more often.

_____

⑤ Sherry doesn't should eat cheese late at night.

_____

42.3 LISTEN TO THE AUDIO AND MARK THE CORRECT ADVICE

Carly should go away to France. ✓
Carly should go away to Finland. ☐

1 Kevin should go out with Jo. ☐
Kevin should go out with Sandra. ☐

2 Paul should wear sun lotion. ☐
Paul should wear a hat. ☐

3 Gabby should go running every day. ☐
Gabby should start a diet. ☐

4 Barry should buy a tie for his grandfather. ☐
Barry should buy socks for his grandfather. ☐

5 Murat should wear a suit for work. ☐
Murat should wear a shirt and tie. ☐

6 Phillip should read some English books. ☐
Phillip should do a language course. ☐

7 Nicky should live with a friend. ☐
Nicky should get a pet. ☐

Aa 42.4 MATCH THE PROBLEMS TO THE CORRECT ADVICE

It's raining.

1 I have no money.

2 I don't speak English well.

3 I can't find a boyfriend.

4 I don't have any nice clothes.

5 I don't have many friends.

6 I want to lose some weight.

7 I can't sleep at night.

8 I can't wake up in the morning.

9 I want to speak perfect French.

10 I want to do well in my exams.

11 I'm feeling very stressed.

You should find a better paid job.

You should do a language course.

You should go get some coffee with my brother.

You should take an umbrella.

You should work hard at school.

You should buy an alarm clock.

You should do something relaxing before bed.

You should go jogging every evening.

You should join some clubs to meet people.

You should take a vacation.

You should live in France for a year.

You should go shopping with me next week.

43 Making suggestions

You can use the modal verb "could" to offer suggestions. "Could" is not as strong as "should." It communicates gentle advice.

✿ **New language** "Could" for suggestions
Aa Vocabulary Advice
✦ **New skill** Making suggestions

43.1 MATCH THE PROBLEMS TO THE CORRECT ADVICE

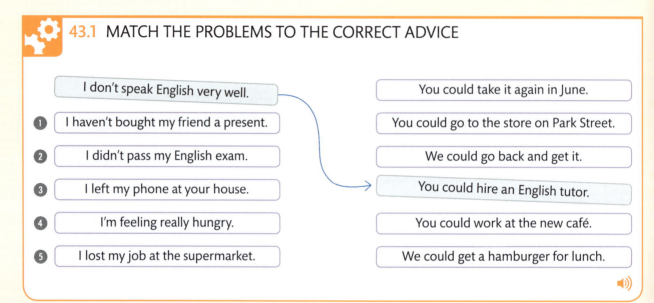

I don't speak English very well. ──────────┐
                                          │
❶ I haven't bought my friend a present.   │   You could take it again in June.

❷ I didn't pass my English exam.   │   You could go to the store on Park Street.

❸ I left my phone at your house.   │   We could go back and get it.

❹ I'm feeling really hungry.   └───▶ You could hire an English tutor.

❺ I lost my job at the supermarket.   You could work at the new café.

                                                 You could take it again in June.
                                                 You could go to the store on Park Street.
                                                 We could go back and get it.
                                                 You could hire an English tutor.
                                                 You could work at the new café.
                                                 We could get a hamburger for lunch.

🔊

43.2 FILL IN THE GAPS USING "COULD" AND THE VERB IN BRACKETS

My lecturer speaks too quickly. You ____*could ask*____ (ask) her to speak more slowly.

❶ My house is too small for my family. You _____ (buy) a bigger house.

❷ Jamal wants to speak better English. He _____ (practice) every day.

❸ I don't know what to do when I finish school. You _____ (apply) to a college.

❹ They don't have jobs right now. They _____ (look) online for a new one.

❺ My sister doesn't like taking the bus. She _____ (learn) to drive herself.

🔊

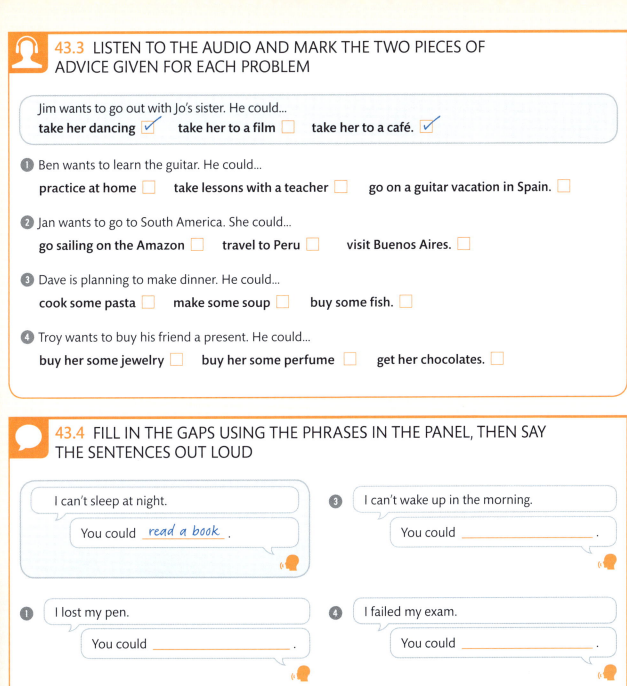

43.3 LISTEN TO THE AUDIO AND MARK THE TWO PIECES OF ADVICE GIVEN FOR EACH PROBLEM

Jim wants to go out with Jo's sister. He could...
take her dancing ☑   **take her to a film** ☐   **take her to a café.** ☑

❶ Ben wants to learn the guitar. He could...
practice at home ☐   **take lessons with a teacher** ☐   **go on a guitar vacation in Spain.** ☐

❷ Jan wants to go to South America. She could...
go sailing on the Amazon ☐   **travel to Peru** ☐   **visit Buenos Aires.** ☐

❸ Dave is planning to make dinner. He could...
cook some pasta ☐   **make some soup** ☐   **buy some fish.** ☐

❹ Troy wants to buy his friend a present. He could...
buy her some jewelry ☐   **buy her some perfume** ☐   **get her chocolates.** ☐

43.4 FILL IN THE GAPS USING THE PHRASES IN THE PANEL, THEN SAY THE SENTENCES OUT LOUD

I can't sleep at night.
You could _read a book_ .

❸ I can't wake up in the morning.
You could _____.

❶ I lost my pen.
You could _____.

❹ I failed my exam.
You could _____.

❷ I don't have a girlfriend.
You could _____.

buy a new one   ~~read a book~~

take it again

buy an alarm clock   go on a blind date

44 Vocabulary

Aa 44.1 HOUSEHOLD CHORES WRITE THE WORDS FROM THE PANEL UNDER THE CORRECT PICTURES

make the bed

1 _____

2 _____

3 _____

4 _____

7 _____

8 _____

9 _____

10 _____

11 _____

14 _____

15 _____

16 _____

17 _____

18 _____

21 _____

22 _____

23 _____

24 _____

25 _____

 5 _____

 6 _____

 12 _____

 13 _____

 19 _____

 20 _____

 26 _____

 27 _____

clean the windows   mop the floor

chop vegetables   set the table

paint a room   do the ironing

clear the table   feed the pets

wash the car   dry the dishes

vacuum the carpet   dust

mend the fence   ~~make the bed~~

hang a picture   buy groceries

walk the dog   sweep the floor

water the plants   do the gardening

scrub the floor   mow the lawn

do the laundry   fold clothes

change the sheets   cook dinner

tidy   load the dishwasher

45 Around the house

You can use the present perfect form of a verb to talk about something that has happened in the past and has consequences in the present.

⚙ **New language** The present perfect
Aa Vocabulary Household chores
🧩 **New skill** Talking about the recent past

Aa **45.1 FIND EIGHT PAST PARTICIPLES IN THE GRID**

```
B C W U C W E T C
C O A F L L W F L
T O S E O C R J E
I K H I S Y L F A
D E E N E W X Q N
I D D J D M E I E
E B S T A R T E D
D P A I N T E D Z
Q P F M W Y Z W S
P W M P A N V F J
S T U D I E D V I
```

study	=	studied
❶ start	=	_____
❷ close	=	_____
❸ tidy	=	_____
❹ clean	=	_____
❺ wash	=	_____
❻ paint	=	_____
❼ cook	=	_____

⚙ **45.2 FILL IN THE GAPS BY PUTTING THE VERBS IN THE PRESENT PERFECT**

Jenny __has watered__ (water) the plants.

❶ Sharon _____ (mow) the lawn.

❷ You _____ (not dust) the living room.

❸ Mike _____ (paint) the walls.

❹ Mom _____ (sail) to France and Italy.

❺ I _____ (mop) the kitchen floor.

❻ He _____ (not cook) the dinner.

❼ They _____ (call) the police.

❽ We _____ (wash) the car.

❾ Jim _____ (change) the sheets.

❿ She _____ (not tidy) her room.

⓫ Karen _____ (visit) Peru.

🔊

45.3 REWRITE THE STATEMENTS AS QUESTIONS

You have washed the car.
Have you washed the car?

1 Charlene has mopped the floor.

_____

2 Sue has changed her sheets.

_____

3 You have cleaned the windows.

_____

4 Hank has tidied his bedroom.

_____

5 Janine has cooked dinner.

_____

6 Mrs. Underwood has visited Ireland.

_____

7 You have started college.

_____

8 Sid has walked to school.

_____

9 She has called her grandmother.

_____

10 You have watched this film.

_____

11 Adam has painted his bedroom.

_____

🔊

45.4 REWRITE THE SENTENCES, CORRECTING THE ERRORS

Greg **haven't** washed his clothes.
Greg hasn't washed his clothes.

1 Katy **haven't** cleaned the bathroom.

_____

2 We **hasn't** left school.

_____

3 I **hasn't** tidied the kitchen.

_____

4 My mom **haven't** read the letter.

_____

5 We **hasn't** painted the backyard fence.

_____

6 James **haven't** tidied his bedroom.

_____

7 You **hasn't** cooked the dinner.

_____

8 Terry **haven't** visited the US.

_____

9 Anne **haven't** been to London.

_____

🔊

45.5 FILL IN THE GAPS BY PUTTING THE VERBS IN THE PRESENT PERFECT

They _____*have left*_____ (leave) the house.

1. Peter _____ (win) the race.

2. We _____ (eat) all the pastries.

3. Michelle _____ (start) a new job.

4. We _____ (finish) our chores.

5. Dave _____ (keep) a seat for you.

6. I _____ (spend) all my money.

7. Chan _____ (break) the window.

8. They _____ (give) Grandpa new slippers.

9. Jacob _____ (hear) the bad news.

10. Mr. Evans _____ (leave) the building.

11. Mike _____ (put) the cup away.

12. He _____ (tell) me about life in the 1960s.

13. Antoine _____ (teach) me French.

14. Craig _____ (write) a novel.

15. Doug _____ (see) that movie twice.

16. We _____ (be) in France for three weeks.

17. Abe _____ (fly) to Paris for the weekend.

18. You _____ (forgot) my birthday again!

19. I _____ (find) a new job.

20. Zac _____ (do) his homework.

21. Hugh _____ (drive) to work today.

22. She _____ (take) her son to school.

23. Owen _____ (buy) a new shirt.

45.6 LISTEN TO THE AUDIO AND ANSWER THE QUESTIONS

Has Sally been to the new café?
Yes, she has. ✓ **No, she hasn't.** ☐

1. Has Peter finished the book?
Yes, he has. ☐ **No, he hasn't.** ☐

2. Have Chloe and Jake finished the report?
Yes, they have. ☐ **No, they haven't.** ☐

3. Has Douglas ever visited Peru?
Yes, he has. ☐ **No, he hasn't.** ☐

4. Has Flo had her lunch?
Yes, she has. ☐ **No, she hasn't.** ☐

5. Has Jenny seen the new spy movie?
Yes, she has. ☐ **No, she hasn't.** ☐

6. Has Peter been to the gym this week?
Yes, he has. ☐ **No, he hasn't.** ☐

7. Has Roger bought a present?
Yes, he has. ☐ **No, he hasn't.** ☐

45.7 FILL IN THE GAPS BY PUTTING THE VERBS IN THE PANEL IN THE PRESENT PERFECT

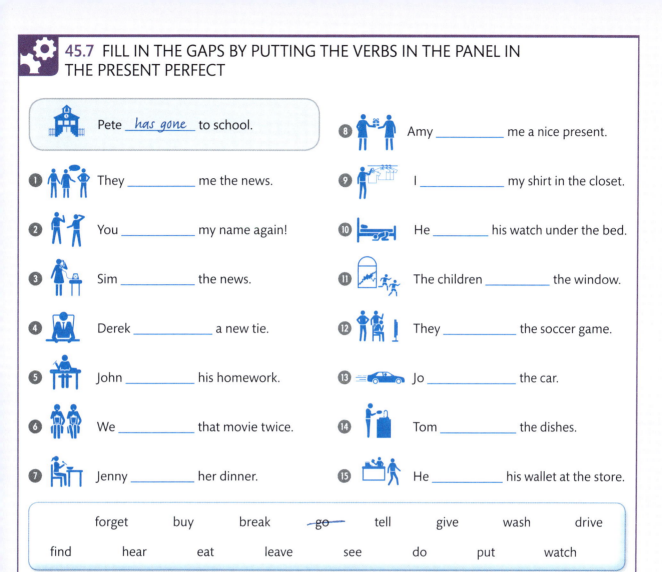

Pete _has gone_ to school.

1 They _____ me the news.

2 You _____ my name again!

3 Sim _____ the news.

4 Derek _____ a new tie.

5 John _____ his homework.

6 We _____ that movie twice.

7 Jenny _____ her dinner.

8 Amy _____ me a nice present.

9 I _____ my shirt in the closet.

10 He _____ his watch under the bed.

11 The children _____ the window.

12 They _____ the soccer game.

13 Jo _____ the car.

14 Tom _____ the dishes.

15 He _____ his wallet at the store.

forget	buy	break	~~go~~	tell	give	wash	drive
find	hear	eat	leave	see	do	put	watch

45.8 USE THE CHART TO CREATE 12 CORRECT SENTENCES AND SAY THEM OUT LOUD

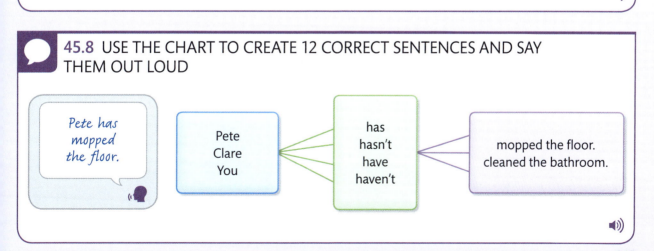

Pete has mopped the floor.

Pete Clare You	has hasn't have haven't	mopped the floor. cleaned the bathroom.

46 Events in your life

Both the present perfect and the past simple can be used to talk about things that happened in the past, but you use them differently.

⚙ **New language** The present perfect
Aa Vocabulary Adventure sports
🧩 **New skill** Talking about past events

46.1 CROSS OUT THE INCORRECT WORDS IN EACH SENTENCE

Logan goes surfing every year. He ~~went~~ / **has been** surfing in Hawaii six times.

❶ **Did you go** / **Have you been** to work yesterday? There was an important meeting at 11 am.

❷ Mom **made** / **has made** a birthday cake for Samantha last weekend. It was delicious.

❸ Owen went to Spain last month. He **sent** / **has sent** us a postcard of Madrid.

❹ I love the film *Trip to Heaven*. I **saw** / **have seen** it five times.

❺ Deena **visited** / **has visited** both the Grand Canyon and Monument Valley in Arizona.

🔊

46.2 RESPOND OUT LOUD TO THE AUDIO USING THE CORRECT TENSES

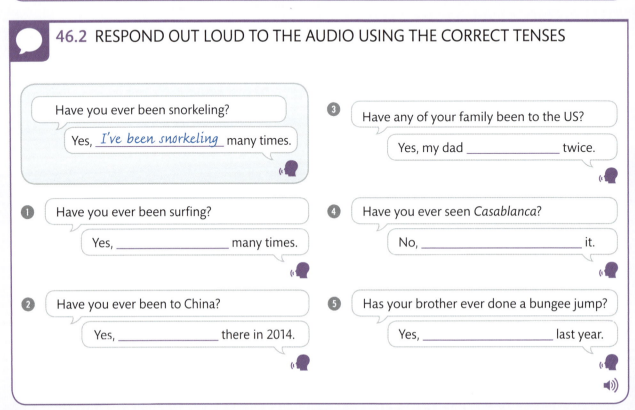

Have you ever been snorkeling?

Yes, *I've been snorkeling* many times.

❶ Have you ever been surfing?

Yes, _____ many times.

❷ Have you ever been to China?

Yes, _____ there in 2014.

❸ Have any of your family been to the US?

Yes, my dad _____ twice.

❹ Have you ever seen *Casablanca*?

No, _____ it.

❺ Has your brother ever done a bungee jump?

Yes, _____ last year.

🔊

Sam went paragliding last summer and in 2013. He __*has been*__ (be) paragliding twice.

1. Fran has been to France many times. She _____ (visit) France last summer.

2. David went rock-climbing in 2013 and 2014. He _____ (be) rock-climbing twice.

3. Cam went bungee-jumping last summer. She _____ (be) bungee-jumping once.

4. Jamie goes surfing most weekends. He _____ (go) surfing yesterday.

5. Rachel climbed Mount Fuji in 2013 and 2014. She _____ (climb) it twice.

6. Jim went diving in Egypt last summer and spring. He _____ (be) diving there twice.

7. I went wing-walking in New Zealand last year. It _____ (be) amazing!

8. My brother went paragliding last summer. He _____ (be) paragliding once.

9. Archie goes snowboarding every winter. He _____ (be) snowboarding eight times.

10. My cousin goes caving most weekends. I _____ (never be) caving.

11. Ray goes windsurfing most weekends. He _____ (go) windsurfing today.

12. My brother loves racing. He _____ (race) in many competitions.

13. I have skied in Austria three times. I _____ (go) skiing there last winter.

14. Tom loves kitesurfing. He _____ (be) kitesurfing in many different countries.

🔊

46.4 READ THE POSTCARD AND WRITE THE VERBS UNDER THE CORRECT HEADINGS

Hi Anna,

We're in New York! We got here four days ago and have seen lots of things. On Tuesday we visited the Statue of Liberty and on Wednesday we went shopping. I have been to Macy's department store, finally! We have had some great food. Last night we ate at a Vietnamese restaurant. It was great. Today we have visited MOMA, the modern art museum. It has been a wonderful trip.

Love,
Harry

PRESENT PERFECT

have seen

1 _____
2 _____
3 _____
4 _____

PAST SIMPLE

got

5 _____
6 _____
7 _____
8 _____

46.5 FILL IN THE GAPS USING "BEEN" OR "GONE"

There's lots of food in the fridge because Ayida's _____been_____ to the supermarket.

1 I love Florence. I've _____ there three times.

2 Tina has _____ to Spain. She'll be back in two weeks.

3 Have you ever _____ skiing in Norway?

4 I've _____ to the new museum in town. It's very crowded.

5 John and Kate have _____ to the theater. They're meeting you there.

6 I have _____ to Hero's to meet some friends. See you there later.

🔊

144

46.6 LISTEN TO THE AUDIO AND ANSWER THE QUESTIONS

Martin and Nigel had a great time in Australia.
True ✓ False ☐ Not given ☐

1 Mary has been to Florida.
True ☐ False ☐ Not given ☐

2 Tony has never visited Paris.
True ☐ False ☐ Not given ☐

3 Sarah went to Japan in 2014.
True ☐ False ☐ Not given ☐

4 Ben has been windsurfing many times.
True ☐ False ☐ Not given ☐

5 Anne has never been to London.
True ☐ False ☐ Not given ☐

6 Steve went paragliding in Portugal.
True ☐ False ☐ Not given ☐

7 Janet has been to Machu Picchu.
True ☐ False ☐ Not given ☐

46.7 FILL IN THE GAPS BY PUTTING THE VERBS IN THE CORRECT TENSES

I _____got_____ (get) my first job five years ago.

1 Larry and Michel _____ (go) to the US twice in 2014.

2 Hannah _____ (dive) in Australia many times.

3 Jim and Rose _____ (make) a cake last weekend.

4 Debbie _____ (never be) to India. She would like to go there one day.

5 Jim _____ (be) to Japan twice. He loved it.

6 I _____ (not try) windsurfing, but I'd like to!

7 Jack _____ (go) to a movie, I'm not sure when he'll be back.

145

Events in your year

One of the uses of the present perfect is to talk about events in a time period that hasn't finished. Use the past simple for a time period that is completed.

⚙ **New language** "Yet" and "already"
Aa Vocabulary Routines and chores
🧩 **New skill** Talking about the recent past

47.1 FILL IN THE GAPS BY PUTTING THE VERBS IN THE PRESENT PERFECT OR PAST SIMPLE

I _____ saw _____ (see) a new movie on Thursday.

1. I _____ (be) to five countries on vacation this year.

2. Sandra _____ (pass) all her medical exams so far this year. I'm so proud.

3. I _____ (visit) Warsaw in 2007 with my family.

4. I'm feeling sleepy. I _____ (not have) any coffee yet this morning.

5. My boyfriend _____ (phone) me last night.

6. Paula's feeling sad. Her dog _____ (die) last week.

7. I'm going to Berlin tomorrow. I _____ (be) there three times before.

8. I don't have any money. I _____ (lose) my wallet yesterday.

9. This is such a good festival. I _____ (make) lots of new friends.

10. My sister is really happy. She _____ (pass) her driving test yesterday.

11. I _____ (play) tennis six times this week. And I'm playing again tomorrow.

🔊

47.2 READ THE ARTICLE AND WRITE ANSWERS TO THE QUESTIONS AS FULL SENTENCES

Where does Rick live?

He lives in Wellington, New Zealand.

1 How many gold medals has Rick won?

_____

2 What happened at the World Championships?

_____

3 When is the next world athletics event?

_____

4 When did Rick first become famous?

_____

5 What has Rick done with his free time?

_____

The long wait

Rick Clay talks about his plans to get back on track

Rick Clay is one of the world's top athletes. He lives in Wellington, New Zealand. Rick has won five gold medals in the last four years. This year has been very difficult for Rick, however. After he injured himself in the World Championships in Athens in June, Rick hasn't run in any more races.

"It's been a very frustrating year. I'm getting better, but it takes time."

The next world athletics event is in Sydney in December. "I really want to go. But I'm not sure if my knee will be ready."

Rick first became famous five years ago when he broke the 400m world record. Rick has tried to be positive about his health problems. "I've done lots of gardening and I've spent more time with my family. So that's good."

 47.3 REWRITE THE SENTENCES, CORRECTING THE ERRORS

I have be to Moscow this year.

I have been to Moscow this year.

1 We has never eaten Chinese food.

_____

2 Sharon have seen that movie before.

_____

3 I have play cricket three times in my life.

_____

4 Natasha has visit Rio de Janeiro three times.

_____

5 Yuri hasn't phone his grandmother.

_____

6 Eddy have bought a new car for his son.

_____

7 Karen is forgotten her ticket for the concert.

_____

Aa 47.4 MATCH THE SENTENCES THAT GO TOGETHER

Have you read this book?

No, the game hasn't started yet.

1 Can you tell Samantha about the party?

I've already told her.

2 Has Rico taken his exam?

He's already arrived.

3 Am I too late for the game?

Yes, I've already read it.

4 What time is Dewain arriving?

It's already landed.

5 I'll order the taxi now.

Sorry, I haven't started it yet.

6 Has the plane from Lisbon landed?

I've already ordered it!

7 Has Claire finished her exercises?

No, he hasn't taken it yet.

8 Have you done your project?

Yes, they've already left.

9 Have Bob and Jane gone back home?

No, she hasn't done them yet.

47.5 LISTEN TO THE AUDIO AND ANSWER THE QUESTIONS

Sue and Jim are getting ready for a party and checking if they have everything.

Jim hasn't made the sandwiches yet.
True ✓ **False** ☐

4 Sue has already bought some wine.
True ☐ **False** ☐

1 Sue has already bought some bread.
True ☐ **False** ☐

5 Jim hasn't bought any juice or soda yet.
True ☐ **False** ☐

2 Sue hasn't bought any ham or cheese yet.
True ☐ **False** ☐

6 Jim has borrowed Danny's wireless speaker.
True ☐ **False** ☐

3 Jim has already bought some avocados.
True ☐ **False** ☐

7 Jim hasn't bought the cake yet.
True ☐ **False** ☐

47.6 FILL IN THE GAPS USING "ALREADY" OR "YET"

The play has _____already_____ started.

① I've _____ read that book.

② I haven't seen the new movie _____ .

③ Chrissie has _____ left for work.

④ The soccer game hasn't started _____ .

⑤ I haven't passed my test _____ .

⑥ I've _____ visited that castle twice.

⑦ Has the party started _____ ?

⑧ I've _____ ordered the taxi.

⑨ Malik has _____ emailed Dan.

⑩ Has Terry cleaned his room _____ ?

⑪ Tony's _____ made the sandwiches.

⑫ I've _____ ordered pizza for everyone.

⑬ Julia hasn't cooked the dinner _____ .

⑭ She hasn't been to London _____ .

⑮ Ali has _____ bought some milk.

⑯ Has Tim phoned his grandmother _____ ?

⑰ Sanjay hasn't sold his car _____ .

◀))

47.7 LOOK AT THE LIST OF CHORES AND WRITE ANSWERS TO THE QUESTIONS USING "ALREADY" OR "YET"

Has Sarah cleaned her room yet?

She's already cleaned her room.

① Has she walked the dog yet?

_____

② Has she sent the emails yet?

_____

③ Has Sarah bought the fruit and vegetables yet?

_____

④ Has she bought a present for Claire yet?

_____

⑤ Has she phoned the bank yet?

_____

TO DO...

~~Clean my room~~
Walk the dog
Send some emails
~~Buy some fruit and vegetables~~
~~Buy a present for Claire~~
Phone the bank

"Eating out" means having a meal outside your home, usually in a restaurant. To do this, you need to know the language for making a reservation and ordering food.

⚙️ **New language** Restaurant phrases
Aa Vocabulary Food preparation
🧩 **New skill** Ordering a meal in a restaurant

Aa 48.1 MATCH THE PICTURES TO THE CORRECT ORDERS

My son would like the tomato soup.

1. I'll have the grilled chicken with salad, please.

2. I'll have the burger and fries, please.

3. For dessert, I'll have the baked banana with cream.

4. To drink, I'd like mineral water, please.

5. I'd like the apple pie and ice cream, please.

6. For my appetizer, I'd like the garlic bread.

7. My daughter would like the carrot cake with yogurt.

48.2 LISTEN TO THE AUDIO AND ANSWER THE QUESTIONS

Two people are ordering food at a restaurant.

The couple have booked a table.
True ✓ **False** ☐

1. The couple ask for a table next to the window.
   True ☐ **False** ☐

2. The couple don't want to see the wine list.
   True ☐ **False** ☐

3. They order when the waiter comes back.
   True ☐ **False** ☐

4. The man orders bean soup.
   True ☐ **False** ☐

5. The woman orders green salad.
   True ☐ **False** ☐

6. The man orders a special.
   True ☐ **False** ☐

7. The woman would like fish.
   True ☐ **False** ☐

8. The couple ask for a bottle of red wine.
   True ☐ **False** ☐

9. The couple both want the same dessert.
   True ☐ **False** ☐

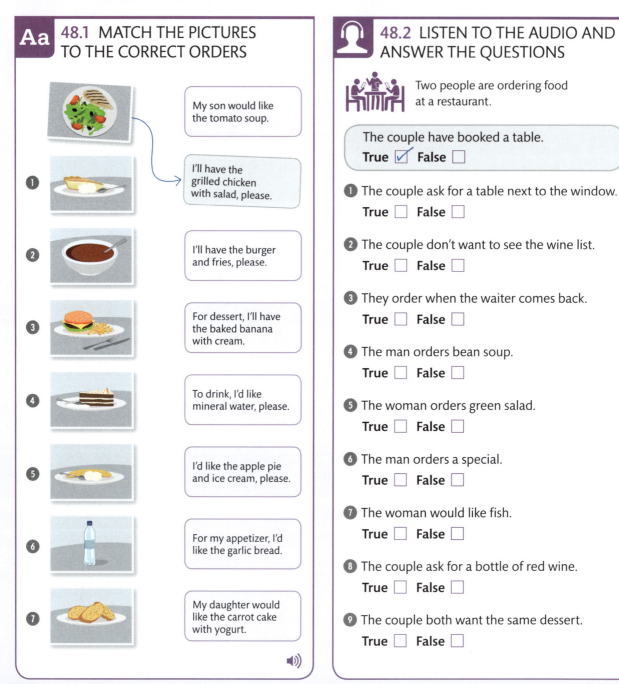

48.3 READ THE MENU AND ANSWER THE QUESTIONS

The restaurant has a separate menu for

Vegetarians ☐
Children ☑
Meat eaters ☐

1 Which appetizer can be shared by two people?

The soup ☐
The salad ☐
The antipasti ☐

2 What do you get with the onion tart?

Garlic bread ☐
New potatoes ☐
Tomato and pepper soup ☐

3 Which of the chef's specials is for vegetarians?

The roast chicken ☐
The fish of the day ☐
The spaghetti ☐

4 How much is the chocolate pudding?

$4.50 ☐
$4.95 ☐
$5.95 ☐

ADAM'S KITCHEN
For children's meals, see separate menu.

APPETIZERS
Roast tomato and pepper soup (V) $3.95
Mediterranean salad with grilled baby vegetables (V) $4.95
Antipasti: Cold meats, cheese, and olives (2 people) $9.95

ENTRÉES
All main courses (not specials) come with new potatoes.
Onion and bean tart with a green salad (V) $7.95
Beef and ale pie with onion gravy $8.95
Spicy pasta with tomato and cheese (V) $6.95

CHEF'S SPECIALS
Whole roast chicken with roast potatoes $8.95
Grilled fish of the day with fries and peas $9.95
Spaghetti with a cream and vegetable sauce (V) $7.95

DESSERTS
Lemon cheesecake $4.50
Chocolate pudding (V) $4.95
Strawberry cake and vanilla ice cream $4.50

(V) = suitable for vegetarians

48.4 USE THE CHART TO CREATE NINE CORRECT SENTENCES AND SAY THEM OUT LOUD

To start, I'll have the tomato soup.

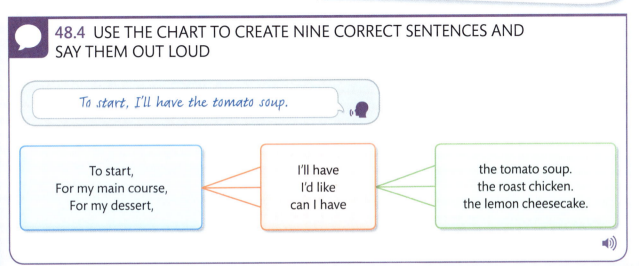

| To start,
For my main course,
For my dessert, | I'll have
I'd like
can I have | the tomato soup.
the roast chicken.
the lemon cheesecake. |

Achievements and ambitions

English uses different forms to talk about future wishes or desires, definite future plans, and past achievements. Use them in conversation to talk about your life.

✿ **New language** Desires and plans
Aa Vocabulary Travel and adventure sports
❖ **New skill** Talking about your achievements

Aa 49.1 MATCH THE QUESTIONS TO THE CORRECT ANSWERS

Questions	Answers
Have you ever been to Kyoto?	Yes, but I prefer rugby.
① Have you ever played soccer?	Yes, I was an English teacher in China.
② Have you ever worked abroad?	Yes, I was on a news program.
③ Have you ever won the lottery?	No, but we're going to Japan next year.
④ Have you ever seen a ghost?	No, I'm scared of heights.
⑤ Have you ever been to Italy?	Yes, it's a really funny movie.
⑥ Have you ever played the piano?	Yes, I saw the Eiffel Tower.
⑦ Have you ever fallen off your bike?	Yes, I love curry.
⑧ Have you ever been on TV?	Yes, when I was at the zoo.
⑨ Have you ever seen a lion?	Yes, I had a cat when I was young.
⑩ Have you ever visited New York?	Yes, I was in Rome last year.
⑪ Have you ever had a pet?	Yes, I once won $10.
⑫ Have you ever been sky diving?	Yes. I was really scared!
⑬ Have you ever seen *Shrek*?	No, but I'd like to see the Statue of Liberty.
⑭ Have you ever been to Paris?	Yes, I played the piano at school.
⑮ Have you ever tried Indian food?	Yes, I broke my arm.

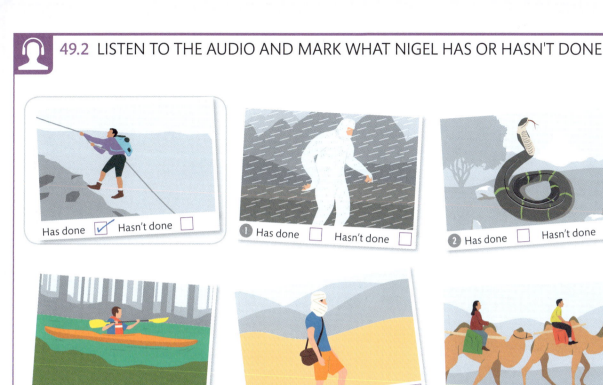

Has done ✓   Hasn't done ☐

① Has done ☐   Hasn't done ☐

② Has done ☐   Hasn't done ☐

③ Has done ☐   Hasn't done ☐

④ Has done ☐   Hasn't done ☐

⑤ Has done ☐   Hasn't done ☐

Aa 49.3 FILL IN THE GAPS USING THE WORDS IN THE PANEL

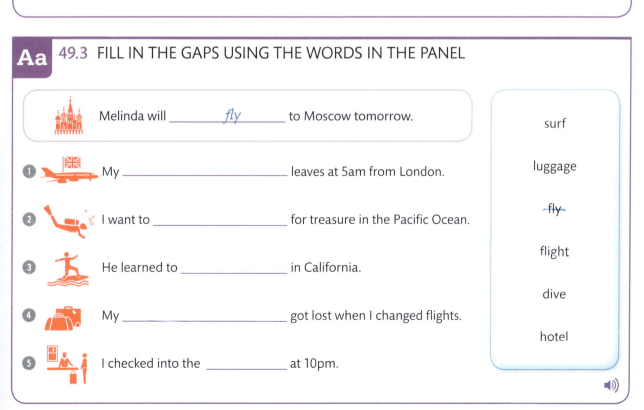

Melinda will _____*fly*_____ to Moscow tomorrow.

① My _____ leaves at 5am from London.

② I want to _____ for treasure in the Pacific Ocean.

③ He learned to _____ in California.

④ My _____ got lost when I changed flights.

⑤ I checked into the _____ at 10pm.

surf

luggage

~~fly~~

flight

dive

hotel

49.4 FILL IN THE GAPS TO SAY WHAT EACH PERSON HASN'T DONE AND WHAT THEY WANT TO DO

Gloria __has never been__ (never / be) to Venice, but she __really wants__ (really / want) to go there.

1. We _____ (never / see) a Shakespeare play, but we _____ (really / want) to see one.

2. Steve _____ (never / play) a musical instrument, but he _____ (really / want) to learn one.

3. I _____ (never / write) a novel, but I _____ (really / want) to do so one day.

4. Esteban _____ (never / eat) Chinese food, but he _____ (really / want) to try some.

5. Ethan _____ (never / see) a wolf, but he _____ (really / want) to photograph one.

6. Stef _____ (never / play) golf, but she _____ (really / want) to try it one day.

7. Tommy _____ (never / be) to America, but he _____ (really / want) to go there.

8. They _____ (never / stay) in a hotel, but they _____ (really / want) to.

9. Doug _____ (never / ride) a horse, but he _____ (really / want) to try it.

10. Marge _____ (never / win) the lottery, but she _____ (really / want) to someday.

11. Kimberley _____ (never / fly) in an airplane, but she _____ (really / want) to do it.

12. Landon _____ (never / climb) a mountain, but he _____ (really / want) to visit the Rockies.

13. Our children _____ (never / be) to a movie theater, but they _____ (really / want) to go.

14. We _____ (never / travel) around South America, but we _____ (really / want) to.

15. Olivia _____ (never / eat) olives, but she _____ (really / want) to try them.

16. I _____ (never / see) an action movie, but I _____ (really / want) to see one.

17. Emily _____ (never / swim) in the ocean, but she _____ (really / want) to try it.

18. Melvin _____ (never / do) a parachute jump, but he _____ (really / want) to do one.

19. Pete _____ (never / see) a tiger, but he _____ (really / want) to travel to India.

20. Patti _____ (never / be) to the theater, but she _____ (really / want) to go.

21. Mary _____ (never / leave) her country, but she _____ (really / want) to travel abroad.

◀))

Aa 49.5 MATCH THE PICTURES TO THE CORRECT SENTENCES

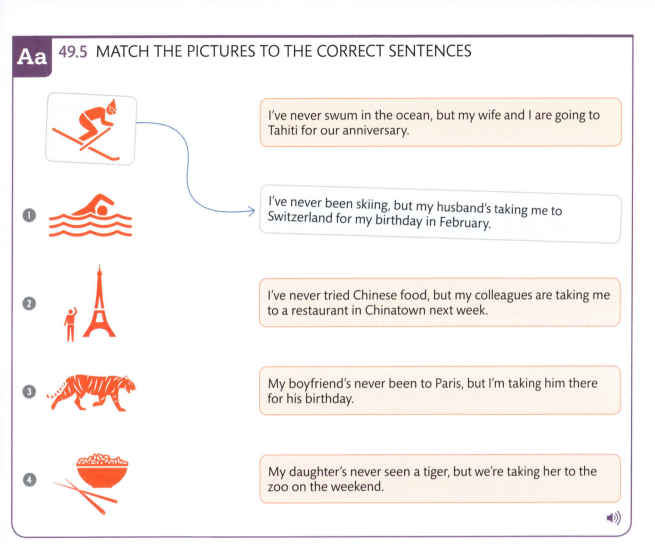

I've never swum in the ocean, but my wife and I are going to Tahiti for our anniversary.

I've never been skiing, but my husband's taking me to Switzerland for my birthday in February.

I've never tried Chinese food, but my colleagues are taking me to a restaurant in Chinatown next week.

My boyfriend's never been to Paris, but I'm taking him there for his birthday.

My daughter's never seen a tiger, but we're taking her to the zoo on the weekend.

49.6 USE THE CHART TO CREATE EIGHT CORRECT SENTENCES AND SAY THEM OUT LOUD

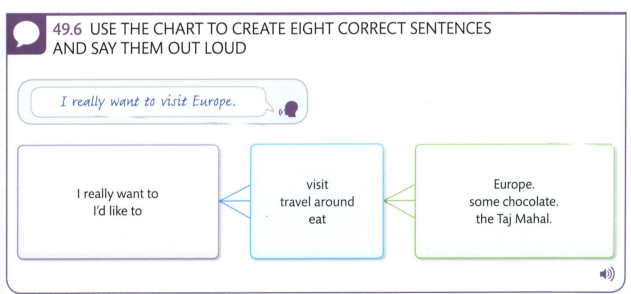

I really want to visit Europe.

I really want to I'd like to	visit travel around eat	Europe. some chocolate. the Taj Mahal.

Answers

01

1.1 🔊
1. They **are** the Walker family.
2. You **are** a police officer.
3. Eve **is** from Canada.
4. I **am** a teacher.
5. We **are** Australian.
6. He **is** an artist.

1.2 🔊
1. They **are** doctors.
2. I **am** from Canada.
3. Elizabeth **is** British.
4. You **are** a mechanic.
5. Luke **is** an engineer.
6. She **is** 35 years old.

1.3 🔊
1. We are French.
2. We are chefs.
3. I am French.
4. She is French.
5. I am Anita.
6. She is Anita.
7. I am an actor.
8. She is an actor.

1.4 🔊 Note: All answers can also be written in contracted form.
1. John and Ellie **are not** best friends.
2. Mr. Robbins **is not** a teacher.
3. It **is not** 2 o'clock.
4. You **are not** my sister.
5. Annabelle **is not** at school.
6. Ann and Ravi **are not** students.
7. Ken **is not** a mechanic.
8. We **are not** doctors.
9. He **is not** 45 years old.
10. They **are not** my teachers.
11. She **is not** from Ireland.
12. It **is not** Martha's book.

1.5 🔊
1. This **is not** the bank.
2. You **are not** a gardener.
3. Selma **is not** a teacher.

4. We **are not** from Spain.
5. I **am not** at home.
6. They **are not** 20 years old.

1.6 🔊
1. **Are** they your dogs?
2. **Is** Jo your cousin?
3. **Is** it 10 o'clock?
4. **Am** I in your class?
5. **Are** you Canadian?
6. **Are** those your keys?
7. **Is** Martin at work today?
8. **Is** Elena 28 years old?
9. **Are** they nurses?

02

2.1 🔊
1. They **cook** pizza for dinner.
2. Your friend **has** a microwave.
3. She **works** at the gym.
4. I **watch** TV every day.
5. We **leave** work at 5pm.
6. Mark **has** a skateboard.
7. They **start** school at 9am.
8. You **hate** soccer.
9. Tara **eats** breakfast at 7:15am.
10. I **go** to the park after work.
11. We **wake up** at 7am.
12. He **cooks** dinner at 8pm.
13. My son **walks** to school.

2.2 🔊
1. Laura **watches** TV all day.
2. You **wake up** at 7am.
3. I **leave** work at 6pm.
4. My cousins **go** to the gym.
5. She **has** a laptop.
6. James **works** in a bank.
7. They **eat** lunch at 1:30pm.

2.3 🔊
1. They **eat** pizza for lunch.
2. Mia **gets up** late on Saturdays.
3. You **go** to work early.
4. We **cook** dinner at 7:30pm.
5. Paul **finishes** work at 6pm.
6. Lily **watches** TV every day.
7. They **start** work at 10am.
8. Robert **has** a car.
9. I **wake up** at 6:45am.
10. Jay **studies** science every day.

11. Karen **likes** tennis.
12. He **works** in a school.
13. Jess **goes** to bed at 10pm.

2.4
A. 4
B. 1
C. 5
D. 2
E. 6
F. 3

2.5
1. False 2. True 3. Not given 4. True
5. True 6. False

2.6 🔊
1. We eat lunch **at 1:30 every day.**
2. Katia wakes up at **6:30 every morning.**
3. My parents have **two cats and a dog.**
4. Dave watches **TV in the evening.**
5. I walk to work **every day.**
6. You work in **an office in town.**

2.7
1. I do not work in a school.
   I don't work in a school.
2. Sam eats lunch at 1pm.
   Sam doesn't eat lunch at 1pm.
3. We leave home at 7:45am.
   We do not leave home at 7:45am.
4. They do not like pizza.
   They don't like pizza.
5. Sia watches TV every day.
   Sia doesn't watch TV every day.
6. My friend has a dog.
   My friend does not have a dog.
7. You do not get up early.
   You don't get up early.
8. I have a new coat.
   I don't have a new coat.
9. He finishes work at 5:30pm.
   He does not finish work at 5:30pm.

2.8 🔊
1. Lucy doesn't walk to work.
2. Lucy doesn't get up early.
3. Lucy doesn't eat breakfast.
4. I don't walk to work.
5. I don't get up early.
6. I don't eat breakfast.
7. They don't walk to work.
8. They don't get up early.
9. They don't eat breakfast.

10. Do you like cats?
11. Do you like soccer?
12. Do you work in an office?
13. Does John like cats?
14. Does John like soccer?
15. Does John work in an office?

03

3.1 🔊
1 Glen **is** cleaning his car.
2 April **is** watching a film.
3 Peter and Frank **are** wearing suits.
4 James **is** painting the kitchen.
5 We **are** traveling around China.
6 You **are** listening to an interesting song.
7 Doug **is** reading a newspaper.

3.2
A 3
B 5
C 1
D 6
E 2
F 4

3.3 🔊
1 Anne **is waiting** for her brother.
2 Pedro **is cooking** pizza for dinner.
3 Mike **is mowing** the lawn.
4 Cynthia **is lying** on the sofa.
5 Jane **is going** to the theater.
6 I **am working** at the moment.
7 Colin **is listening** to some music.
8 Our children **are playing** in a band.
9 We **are drinking** lemonade.
10 Stefan **is coming** to our party.
11 They **are eating** pasta for dinner.
12 Roberta **is wearing** a sweater.
13 You **are playing** tennis with John.

3.4 🔊
1 Paula doesn't often watch TV, **but tonight she's watching a good movie.**
2 Sven usually cooks at home, **but today he's eating at a restaurant.**
3 I often go to bed at 11pm, **but this evening I'm going to bed early.**
4 Janet is working at home today, **but she usually works in an office.**
5 Ravi usually wears casual clothes, **but today he's wearing a business suit.**

6 Tim usually has cereal for breakfast, **but this morning he's having eggs.**
7 We usually go on vacation to Greece, **but this year we're visiting Italy.**
8 I almost always drive to work, **but today I'm walking as my car won't start.**
9 Nelson is drinking wine today, **but he normally drinks beer.**
10 You usually wear pants, **but today you're wearing a skirt.**

3.5 🔊
1 Vlad **isn't** playing soccer.
2 We **aren't** working today.
3 Manek **isn't** wearing a tie.
4 We **aren't** coming to the party.
5 Clarice **isn't** having dinner today.
6 Jonathan **isn't** walking the dog.
7 Mark and Trevor **aren't** going to the theater.
8 Pedro **isn't** wearing a suit.
9 Sally and Clive **aren't** going on vacation.
10 Sebastian **isn't** watching the movie.
11 You **aren't** working hard enough.

3.6 🔊
1 Angelica isn't watching TV.
2 I'm working at home.
3 We aren't playing soccer.
4 Ginny is eating a burger.
5 Sharon isn't listening to music.
6 They are drinking soda.
7 We aren't going shopping.
8 Anita is visiting Athens.
9 Pete isn't playing tennis.
10 You are speaking Dutch.
11 Paul isn't wearing a hat.
12 I am walking home.
13 Steven isn't going swimming.

3.7 🔊
1 Kate isn't going on vacation this year.
2 Tracy is taking the dog for a walk.
3 Irena isn't coming to the party.
4 We are walking to school today.
5 Trevor is cooking his dinner.
6 Mr. Smith is traveling to Singapore.
7 They aren't playing soccer today.
8 I am buying a new pair of shoes.
9 You aren't wearing a coat today.

3.8 🔊
1 Jenny is wearing pants.
2 Gemma isn't driving to work.
3 We are singing.
4 Brendan is eating a burger.
5 Sal is wearing a long coat.
6 Mo is watching a movie.
7 Emily is wearing glasses.
8 Jo is listening to music.
9 Kate is wearing a skirt.

04

4.1 🔊
1 What is he reading? **A book.**
2 Where are you going? **To the library.**
3 Who is talking? **Sue and Johnny.**
4 Why is she shouting? **She's angry.**
5 What is he wearing? **A suit and tie.**
6 What are the children doing? **Playing computer games.**

4.2 🔊
1 Lenny is **wearing** a tie today.
2 Sarah is **cooking** dinner.
3 Frank is **running** in the park.
4 Jane is **walking** the dog.
5 Simon is **listening** to music.
6 Pat is **driving** to work.
7 Gavin is **eating** breakfast.

4.3
1 Diane
2 Tommy
3 Jo
4 Alex
5 Jean
6 George
7 Isabel
8 Ray
9 Louise
10 Jon

4.4 🔊
1 I **am doing** my English homework.
2 He **is making** breakfast.
3 She **is reading** a magazine.
4 They **are running** by the river.
5 I **am writing** an email.
6 We **are listening** to music.
7 She **is driving** to London.
8 He **is taking** a bath.

9 They **are doing** the shopping.
10 I **am eating** a pizza.
11 You **are riding** a motorcycle.
12 We **are going** to bed.

4.5 🔊
1 What is Kay watching?
2 What is Dan eating?
3 What are Tim and Jay playing?
4 What is Sara wearing?
5 What are you carrying?
6 What is Charlie listening to?
7 What is Sharon drinking?
8 What is Sam making?
9 What are you writing?

4.6 🔊
1 Where is Kim going?
2 Who are you phoning?
3 Why are you crying?
4 When are you meeting John?
5 What are you cooking?
6 Where is your band playing?
7 Why are you shouting?
8 What are you drinking?
9 How are you getting to the concert?

4.7
1 Claude
2 Robert
3 Peter's mom
4 Pedro
5 Dan

4.8 🔊
1 **They are drinking** some coffee.
2 **Meg is eating** a pizza.
3 **Louise is riding** a horse.
4 **Paul is using** his computer.
5 **Philippa is baking** a cake.

05

5.1
ACTION VERBS
eat, sing, learn, play, go, listen
STATE VERBS
have, love, want, remember, know, hate

5.2 🔊
1 I remember it is your birthday today.
2 Dan wants a drink.

3 You have two sisters.
4 He owns this house.
5 My brother loves Anne.
6 We own a horse.
7 My dad hates pizza.

5.3 🔊
1 Greg **is playing** tennis now.
2 Mo **is watching** TV right now.
3 We **have** a new dog.
4 You **don't like** snakes.
5 Dom **is going** to school now.

5.4
1 Jane **works** at the school near her apartment.
2 Jane really **likes** teaching.
3 Jane **goes** to restaurants on the weekend.
4 Jane **has** three children.
5 Ben **is playing** soccer with his friends.
6 Silvia **is watching** a film at the movie theater.
7 Mike **is listening** to music in his room.

5.5 🔊
1 Samantha has three children.
2 They're running to school.
3 She hates snakes.
4 She's listening to music.

06

6.1 🔊
1 stressed
2 lonely
3 unhappy
4 bored
5 curious
6 distracted
7 angry
8 worried
9 tired
10 jealous
11 excited
12 calm
13 relaxed
14 confident
15 disappointed
16 scared
17 grateful
18 amused
19 irritated

20 confused
21 proud
22 surprised
23 anxious

07

7.1
excited, nervous, bored, pleased, bad, calm, happy, sad, angry, tired

7.2 🔊
1 Alexander is feeling **excited**.
2 Danny is feeling **tired**.
3 Peter is feeling **proud**.
4 Samantha is feeling **sad**.
5 I'm feeling **happy**.
6 Christopher is feeling **curious**.
7 Waldo is feeling **bored**.

7.3 🔊
1 Claire is feeling happy because it's her birthday.
2 Marge is feeling annoyed because Jack is being naughty.
3 Shaun is feeling excited because he's watching soccer.
4 Chris is feeling tired because it's very late.
5 Angelo is feeling bored because his book isn't interesting.
6 Sandy is feeling jealous because her sister has a new toy.
7 Rachel is feeling nervous because she has an exam.
8 Carl is feeling sad because he misses his dog.
9 Anne is feeling angry because her boyfriend is late.
10 Jimmy is feeling pleased because he has a new car.
11 Ron is feeling relaxed because he is on vacation.

7.4 🔊
1. I am feeling nervous.
2. I am feeling happy.
3. I am feeling sad.
4. Jim is feeling nervous.
5. Jim is feeling happy.
6. Jim is feeling sad.
7. We are feeling nervous.
8. We are feeling happy.
9. We are feeling sad.

10. They are feeling nervous.

11. They are feeling happy.

12. They are feeling sad.

7.5

1 Charles is feeling scared.

2 Colin is feeling sad.

3 Jim is feeling nervous.

4 Greg is feeling annoyed.

5 Tanya is feeling tired.

6 Bill and Susan are feeling excited.

7 Giles is feeling happy.

8 Arnold is feeling relaxed.

9 Katy is feeling bored.

7.6 🔊

1 Evie is really angry. **The bus still hasn't arrived.**

2 Peter is feeling very tired today. **So he's staying in bed.**

3 Jenny is so nervous. **She has an exam tomorrow.**

4 Danny is feeling really dissapointed. **He didn't win the competition.**

5 Angelo is so bored. **He wants something to do.**

7.7 🔊

1 It's my birthday tomorrow. I really can't wait! I'm so **excited**.

2 I don't like this house. It's so dark. Is that a spider? I'm feeling very **scared**.

3 I don't know what to do. There's nothing on TV. I'm really **bored**.

4 This book is really depressing. So many bad things happen. I'm feeling really **sad**.

5 My girlfriend's forgotten my birthday. And she forgot last year. I'm so **angry**.

08

8.1 🔊

1 boat

2 train station

3 port

4 taxi rank

5 fly a plane

6 fare

7 ride a bike

8 ticket

9 helicopter

10 bus

11 walk

12 tram

13 taxi

14 plane

15 car

16 drive a car

17 airport

18 steering wheel

19 yacht

20 bus stop

21 ship

22 road

23 train

09

9.1 🔊

1 Tony often **goes** for a swim in the evening, but today he **is visiting** a friend.

2 Today Baz **is having** eggs, but he mostly **eats** cereal for breakfast.

3 John's sister usually **drives** to work, but today she **is walking**.

4 Clara usually **sleeps** in the afternoon, but today she **is going** for a walk.

5 My cousins often **play** soccer together, but today they **are playing** golf.

6 He normally **goes** on vacation to Peru, but this year he **is visiting** Greece.

7 Jenny usually **watches** TV in the evening, but tonight she **is reading**.

8 Abe often **plays** soccer on Fridays, but today he **is watching** a game.

9 Tonight our dog **is sleeping** in the kitchen, but he often **sleeps** outside.

10 Liza usually **goes** to the gym after work, but today she **is resting**.

11 They often **go** running on Saturdays, but today they **are shopping**.

9.2 🔊

1 My wife usually **works** until 5pm, but this evening she **is working** until 7:30pm.

2 Jim often **listens** to the radio in the evening, but tonight he **is going** to a party.

3 I often **meet** my friends in the evening, but tonight I **am meeting** my grandmother.

4 Mrs. Brown **is teaching** English this week, but she normally **teaches** geography.

5 Hank **is walking** in the Pyrenees this week, but he usually **goes** to work every day.

9.3 🔊

1 I normally **go** to bed at 11pm, but tonight I **am meeting** some friends.

2 Today Jane **is eating** a sandwich, but she often **has** soup for lunch.

3 Sam usually **drinks** coffee, but this morning he **is drinking** tea.

4 Tonight we **are having** water with our dinner, but we usually **have** juice.

5 I usually **feel** confident about exams, but today I **am feeling** nervous.

10

10.1 🔊

1 ankle

2 arm

3 eyelashes

4 chest

5 fingers

6 lips

7 heel

8 chin

9 ear

10 head

11 toes

12 cheek

13 eyebrow

14 shin

15 thumb

16 tooth

17 knee

18 hair

19 nose

20 fingernail

21 face

22 hand

23 thigh

24 neck

25 knuckles

26 foot

27 leg

28 eye

29 teeth

30 stomach

31 shoulders

11

11.1 🔊

1 I **am not** feeling well today. I'm sorry. Let's meet next week instead.
2 May and Clara are **feeling** sick today. They're going to stay at home.
3 Cathy **isn't** feeling well. She is not going swimming today.
4 Jerry is **feeling** really sick, but he's still going to work.
5 We don't **feel** well, so we aren't coming to the party tonight.
6 Alexander **doesn't** feel well. He's going to stay at home today.
7 They don't **feel** well. They're not going to visit their uncle and aunt today.
8 Hilary isn't **feeling** well. She can't come to the movies tonight.
9 Lee **feels** sick. He can't come to the sales meeting today.
10 John and Diana **are** not feeling well. They are going to leave work early today.

11.2 🔊

1 I can't hear and I have an earache.
2 Dan's leg hurts.
3 Maria has a broken leg.
4 I don't feel well. I have a stomachache.
5 Claire has a terrible headache.
6 I have a pain in my knee.
7 Philip can't stand. He has backache.

11.3

1 False 2 True 3 False 4 True
5 Not given 6 True 7 False

11.4 🔊

1. I have a broken leg.
2. I have a pain in my foot.
3. I have a headache.
4. I have got a broken leg.
5. I have got a pain in my foot.
6. I have got a headache.
7. You have got a broken leg.
8. You have got a headache.
9. You have a broken leg.
10. You have a headache.
11. Anna has a broken leg.
12. Anna has a headache.

12

12.1 🔊

1 hot
2 boiling
3 cold
4 freezing
5 rain
6 snow
7 hail
8 thunder
9 humidity
10 flood
11 puddle
12 blue sky
13 cloud
14 lightning
15 rainbow
16 temperature
17 sun
18 ice
19 tornado
20 wind
21 gale
22 dry
23 wet

13

13.1 🔊

1 The weather here is horrible! It's raining all the time. It's cold and wet.
2 It's boiling here. It's too hot to go out in the middle of the day.
3 It's a sunny day and there's lots of snow. It's perfect weather for skiing.
4 It's freezing here. It's too cold to stay outdoors for very long.
5 It's a really windy day here. I'm going windsurfing later today.
6 The weather here is very stormy. Last night we had lots of lightning.
7 There were icicles on the house this morning. It's very cold here.

13.2 🔊

1 It's very windy.
2 It's very rainy.
3 It's very snowy.
4 It's very sunny.
5 It's very stormy.
6 It's very icy.
7 It's very cloudy.
8 It's very stormy.
9 It's very misty.

13.3 🔊

1 Be careful. There's **ice** on the road.
2 The weather's beautiful. It's hot and **sunny**.
3 It's quite **warm** here. The temperature is 68°F.
4 It's 14°F here and it's snowy. It's **freezing**.
5 Oh no, it's **raining**. We can't play tennis now.
6 It's very **foggy**. The airport is closed.
7 There's a **storm**. We can't play golf.

13.4

1 Spain
2 London
3 Lisbon
4 Sweden
5 France

13.5 🔊

1. There's a lot of rain at the moment.
2. There's a lot of rain in London today.
3. There's a lot of sun at the moment.
4. There's a lot of sun in London today.
5. It's really warm at the moment.
6. It's really warm in London today.
7. It's really freezing at the moment.
8. It's really freezing in London today.
9. It's quite warm at the moment.
10. It's quite warm in London today.

14

14.1 🔊

1 get on a bus
2 miss a flight
3 go sightseeing
4 apartment
5 passport control
6 arrive at the airport
7 pack your bags
8 luggage
9 reception
10 road trip
11 get off a bus
12 cruise
13 board a plane
14 arrive at a hotel

⑮ on time
⑯ boarding card
⑰ runway
⑱ hostel
⑲ security
⑳ late
㉑ fly in a plane
㉒ leave a hotel
㉓ hand luggage

15

15.1 ◄))
❶ I'm **taller** than you are.
❷ A train is **faster** than a bus.
❸ 79°F is **hotter** than 64°F.
❹ A car is faster than a **bike**.
❺ **France** is smaller than Russia.
❻ Everest is higher than **Mont Blanc**.
❼ 6am is **earlier** than 9am.
❽ A tiger is **bigger** than a pig.
❾ Your dress is **prettier** than mine.
❿ 95°F is **colder** than 110°F.
⓫ The Sahara is **hotter** than the Arctic.
⓬ 11pm is **later** than 3pm.
⓭ An **elephant** is bigger than a mouse.
⓮ A plane is **faster** than a car.
⓯ **Ice cream** is colder than milk.
⓰ Mars is **closer** to earth than Pluto.
⓱ Athens is **older** than Los Angeles.

15.2
❶ thinner
❷ easier
❸ later
❹ dirtier
❺ larger
❻ bigger
❼ hotter
❽ lower

15.3 ◄))
❶ This painting is beautiful. It's **more beautiful than** that one.
❷ Russian is very difficult. It's **more difficult than** Italian.
❸ Rome is very old. It's **older than** my city.
❹ Pizza is very tasty. It's **tastier than** pasta.
❺ China is very large. It's **larger than** Germany.
❻ Oslo is very cold. It's **colder than** Paris.
❼ Science is very difficult. It's **more difficult than** geography.

❽ Monaco is very expensive. It's **more expensive than** Berlin.
❾ Mountain climbing is dangerous. It's **more dangerous than** hiking.
❿ This book is very interesting. It's **more interesting than** yours.
⓫ Skiing is exciting. It's **more exciting than** jogging.

15.4
❶ False ❷ False ❸ True
❹ False ❺ True

15.5 ◄))
❶ Flying is **safer than** driving.
Driving is **more dangerous than** flying.
❷ My computer is **older than** my phone.
My phone is **newer than** my computer.
❸ The suitcase is **heavier than** the bag.
The bag is **lighter than** the suitcase.
❹ This champagne is **more expensive than** that wine.
This wine is **cheaper than** that champagne.
❺ 118°F is **hotter than** 90°F.
90°F is **colder than** 118°F.

15.6 ◄))
❶ 11pm **is later than** 10pm.
❷ Gold **is cheaper than** platinum.
❸ Athens **is older than** Los Angeles.
❹ Chess **is more difficult than** poker.
❺ Tennis **is more energetic than** walking.

15.7 ◄))
❶ Spain **is hotter than** England.
❷ Juice **is more expensive than** water.
❸ 10pm **is later than** 6pm.
❹ Norway **is colder than** Egypt.
❺ The tortoise **is slower than** the cheetah.

16

16.1 ◄))
❶ The Great Wall of China is the **longest** wall in the world.
❷ The African Bush Elephant is the **biggest** land animal.
❸ Vatican City is the **smallest** country in the world.
❹ The Burj Khalifa is the **tallest** building in the world.
❺ The Amazon is the **widest** river in the world.

❻ Dolphins are in the top 10 **most intelligent** animals.

16.2
❶ smallest
❷ biggest
❸ farthest / furthest
❹ highest
❺ thinnest
❻ fattest
❼ most beautiful
❽ ugliest
❾ cleanest
❿ dirtiest
⓫ most expensive
⓬ newest
⓭ oldest
⓮ most intelligent
⓯ fastest

16.3
❶ Sue
❷ Jane
❸ Dan
❹ Jane
❺ Jane
❻ Jane
❼ Dan

16.4 ◄))
❶ A rhino is heavier than a lion, but elephants are the **heaviest** land animal.
❷ A whale is more intelligent than a shark, but dolphins are the **most intelligent** sea animal.
❸ The Regal is more expensive than the Grand, but the Plaza is the **most expensive** hotel.
❹ The Statue of Liberty is taller than the Leaning Tower of Pisa, but Big Ben is the **tallest**.
❺ The Thames is longer than the Trent, but the Severn is the **longest** river in the UK.

16.5
❶ the most expensive
❷ the most comfortable
❸ the most intelligent
❹ the most dangerous
❺ the most exciting
❻ the most impressive
❼ the most handsome

16.6

1 The Rialto
2 The Grand
3 The Plaza
4 The Grand
5 The Plaza
6 The Rialto

16.7 🔊

1 The Amazon rainforest has some of the **most beautiful** plants in the world.
2 Mesopotamia is thought to be the home of the **earliest** civilization in the world.
3 The British Museum is the **most popular** tourist attraction in the UK.
4 New York City and Geneva are the **most expensive** cities in the world.
5 Hippopotamuses are one of the world's **most dangerous** animals.

16.8 🔊

1 The Shanghai Tower is a very tall building. It is **the tallest building** in China.
2 The sloth is a very slow animal. It is **the slowest animal** in the world.
3 The Vasco da Gama bridge in Portugal is very long. It is **the longest bridge** in Europe.
4 The Dead Sea is a very low point on Earth. It is **the lowest point** on Earth.
5 Mount Elbrus in Russia is a very tall mountain. It is **the tallest mountain** in Europe.

17

17.1 🔊

1 coast
2 iceberg
3 rainforest
4 ocean
5 hill
6 canyon
7 swamp
8 island
9 countryside
10 valley
11 cave
12 pond
13 mountain
14 beach
15 waterfall
16 polar region

17 volcano
18 river
19 oasis
20 woods
21 cliff
22 rocks
23 desert

18

18.1 🔊

1 Would you like to stay in **and** watch a DVD tonight?
2 Do you want to go to the Tower of London **or** the London Eye?
3 Do you want pizza **or** salad for dinner tonight?
4 Is Marianne a pop singer **and** a modern jazz singer?
5 Can I pay for the washing machine in cash **or** by credit card?
6 On birthdays, we open our presents **and** play party games.
7 Do you want to go to a movie **or** the theater tomorrow night?
8 Would you like to study French **and** German next year?
9 Did you live in a house **or** an apartment when you were in Thailand?
10 I had coffee **and** chocolate cake at the new café in town.
11 Would you like tea **or** coffee while you wait for your appointment?

18.2 🔊

1 **Which** is Tom's car, the red or the blue one?
2 **What** is the biggest country in Europe?
3 **Which** is bigger, a lion or a hippo?
4 **Which** would you like? Cake or cookies?
5 **What** would you like to do this evening?
6 **What** shall we have for dinner tonight?
7 **Which** ink does he use, black or blue?
8 **What** is your favorite food?
9 **What** is the tallest mountain in the world?

18.3 🔊

1 **What** would you like to do tomorrow when we meet?
2 **What** is the fastest animal in the world?
3 **Which** restaurant would you like to go to, the Italian or the Indian one?

4 **Which** language does he speak, French, Italian, or Spanish?
5 **What** is your favorite subject at school?
6 **Which** of these houses does Mike live in?

18.4 🔊

1 My exam results were **worse** than Frank's.
2 The Plaza is the **best** hotel in the city.
3 My new workplace is **farther / further** from my house than my old one.
4 I am a **better** driver than my brother.
5 Don't go to Gigi's. It's the **worst** café in town.
6 Neptune is the **farthest / furthest** planet from the Sun.

18.5 🔊

1 My brother is worse at soccer than I am.
2 The blue T-shirt is more expensive than the red T-shirt.
3 Harry's café is better than Gino's café.
4 I am worse than my sister at languages.
5 The blue pen is less expensive / cheaper than the red pen.

18.6

1 The food in Paris is better than the food at home.
2 Pat ate the best meal at La Coupole.
3 The Eiffel Tower is the tallest building in Paris.
4 You can hear the best music in Paris at Le Pompon.
5 The Mona Lisa is the most famous painting in the Louvre.

18.7 🔊

1 Rhode Island **is the smallest** state in the US.
2 The Humber Bridge **is longer** than the Severn Bridge.
3 George **is the worst** student in the class.
4 A Ferrari **is more expensive** than a Fiat car.
5 Saturn **is farther / further** from Earth than Mars.

19

19.1

1 8,624
2 3,499,000
3 496,632

4 3,735,000
5 15,265
6 1,537,895

19.2 🔊

1 Seven thousand, three hundred and ninety-six
2 Thirty-four thousand, nine hundred and seventy-five
3 Two hundred and twelve thousand, four hundred and fifty-seven
4 Fifteen million, seven hundred and ninety-five thousand
5 Twenty-six million, six hundred and fifty-five thousand, eight hundred and seventy-two
6 Forty-seven million, two hundred and twenty-nine thousand, two hundred and eighty-six
7 Fifty-three million, one hundred and ninety-eight thousand, five hundred and thirty-eight

19.3 🔊

1 455,058
2 564,143
3 3,682
4 45,712,600
5 63,859
6 950,837
7 23,100,269
8 978
9 185,794
10 50,212,705
11 10,460,240
12 336,422
13 16,703
14 1,359,607

19.4

1 453
2 987
3 15,678
4 28,761
5 73,547
6 195,326
7 361,216
8 548,972
9 932,671
10 1,295,634
11 3,940,522
12 6,457,815
13 10,430,695
14 16,852,794

20

20.1 🔊

1 Sunday
2 Monday
3 Tuesday
4 Wednesday
5 Thursday
6 Friday
7 day
8 week
9 fortnight
10 month
11 February
12 April
13 July
14 August
15 September
16 November
17 December
18 summer
19 winter

20.2 🔊

1 nineteenth
2 twenty-sixth
3 fifth
4 sixth
5 twenty-ninth
6 twenty-first
7 sixteenth
8 twenty-seventh
9 seventeenth
10 tenth
11 fourteenth
12 first
13 eleventh
14 twentieth
15 twenty-third
16 thirty-first
17 seventh
18 third
19 fourth

21

21.1

1 We returned on the 9th of September.
2 Sarah was born on March 12.
3 Greg was born on the 12th of February.

4 My birthday is on November 22.
5 I stop working on the 21st of July.
6 The year begins on January 1.

21.2

1 is not at work.
2 is going to Los Angeles.
3 is busy all day.

21.3

1 True **2** False **3** Not given
4 False **5** True **6** True **7** False

21.4 🔊

1. My wedding is on February 16.
2. My wedding is on the 16th of February.
3. Sharon's wedding is on February 16.
4. Sharon's wedding is on the 16th of February.
5. He was born five years ago.
6. He was born 25 years ago.
7. Peter was born five years ago.
8. Peter was born 25 years ago.

22

22.1 🔊

1 Roberta **was** at the party last night.
2 We **were** in college together.
3 You **were** a student at that time.
4 There **were** lots of people in town.
5 They **were** there in the evening.
6 Your friends **were** at the museum yesterday.
7 She **was** a teacher in the 1970s.
8 There **was** a café near the beach.
9 My mom **was** a dentist.
10 Chris and I **were** happy about the news.
11 They **were** at the theater last night.
12 Frank **was** an actor in the 1990s.
13 It **was** very cold in Norway.
14 My parents **were** away last week.
15 We **were** in Los Angeles in 2014.
16 You **were** at the movie theater on Friday.
17 Jenny **was** a nurse for 20 years.

22.2

1 1960s
2 1910s
3 1490s
4 1605

22.3
① False ② False ③ True ④ True
⑤ False ⑥ False ⑦ True ⑧ True
⑨ False ⑩ False

22.4 🔊
① It **wasn't** an interesting book.
② There **weren't** any good movies on.
③ We **weren't** in the US in 2012.
④ Glen **wasn't** at home when I called.
⑤ There **wasn't** a theater in my town.
⑥ Trevor **wasn't** in Berlin in 1994.
⑦ There **wasn't** a library in the town.
⑧ We **weren't** at home last night.
⑨ Peter **wasn't** a student at Harvard.
⑩ Carlo **wasn't** very good at singing.
⑪ Meg and Clive **weren't** teachers then.
⑫ They **weren't** at the restaurant last night.

22.5 🔊
① Brad **wasn't** a teacher in 2012.
② The weather **wasn't** bad.
③ It **wasn't** a comfortable bed.
④ They **weren't** interesting people.
⑤ Brendan's parents **weren't** doctors.
⑥ Pete and Sue **weren't** on the beach all day.

22.6 🔊
① Simon was an actor for 30 years.
② It was really cold in Canada.
③ Were there any stores in the town?
④ Phil wasn't good at dancing.
⑤ Was Rebecca in Arizona in 2010?

22.7 🔊
① Was she at school in the nineties?
② Were you at the park last Sunday?
③ Were there lots of people at his party?
④ Was he very good at playing soccer?
⑤ Was James at work until 8 o'clock yesterday?
⑥ Were you at the airport before me?
⑦ Were they at Simon's wedding last week?
⑧ Were we in Spain for two weeks?
⑨ Was Hayley happy in college?

22.8 🔊
1. Was she a teacher?
2. Was she angry?
3. Was she at home yesterday?
4. Was there a party last night?
5. Were they angry?
6. Were you angry?
7. Were you a teacher?
8. Were they at home yesterday?
9. Were you at home yesterday?

23

23.1 🔊
① Roger **watched** the game.
② They **called** their dad yesterday.
③ We **arrived** at the hotel at 7pm.
④ They **walked** to school yesterday.
⑤ Simon **worked** late last week.
⑥ My mother **danced** at the party.
⑦ They **washed** their new car.
⑧ Terry **studied** French at school.
⑨ Karen **traveled** to Africa.

23.2
① Craig **phoned** his girlfriend.
② The doctor **didn't visit** my grandmother.
③ We **played** tennis last night.
④ My sister **didn't walk** to the shops.
⑤ They **watched** TV last night.
⑥ Debbie **didn't move** to the US this year.
⑦ David **cleaned** his room again.

23.3 🔊
① Kelly **watched** TV last night.
② Tim **walked** home on Friday.
③ Ed **worked** as a waiter last year.
④ I **tried** some Mexican food.
⑤ Marge **called** her sister last night.
⑥ Marion **played** some music.
⑦ The children **asked** a question.
⑧ My dad **lived** in Canada.
⑨ They **remembered** my birthday.

23.4
VERBS THAT TAKE "ED":
① washed ② started ③ visited
VERBS THAT TAKE "IED":
④ studied ⑤ carried ⑥ tried
VERBS THAT TAKE "D":
⑦ danced ⑧ arrived ⑨ moved

23.5 🔊
① I **studied** English.
② Jim **arrived** today.
③ My son **carried** my bags.
④ She **danced** very well.
⑤ Bill **washed** his socks.

23.6
① cleaned her kitchen.
② watched TV with her boyfriend.
③ visited her grandmother.
④ danced at a party.

23.7
① Peter changed schools when **he was six years old.**
② Peter finished school when **he was 18 years old.**
③ He started college when **he was 19.**
④ Peter worked in a bookstore when **he was 20.**
⑤ He moved to France when **he was 25 years old.**
⑥ He met his future wife when **he was 26 years old.**
⑦ Peter and Joanne married when **he was 28.**
⑧ Their first child was born when **Peter was 30.**
⑨ They visited Australia when **Peter was 32.**
⑩ He started his own company when **he was 33.**
⑪ They moved when **he was 35.**
⑫ Their second child was born when **Peter was 37.**

23.8 🔊
1. I lived in France when I was young.
2. I worked in a cafe when I was young.
3. I visited Spain when I was young.
4. James lived in France when he was in college.
5. James worked in a cafe when he was in college.
6. James visited Spain when he was in college.
7. Carol lived in France when she was in college.
8. Carol worked in a cafe when she was in college.
9. Carol visited Spain when she was in college.

24

24.1
① Carl **could** run fast.
② Brendan **could** speak five languages.
③ Sally **could** paint beautifully.
④ Rob and Sarah **couldn't** dance flamenco.
⑤ Yasmin **could** climb a tree.

6 Danny **could** drive a bus.
7 We **couldn't** ride a horse.
8 Jenny **could** play the violin.
9 Ben **could** fly a plane.
10 Yuna **could** speak Italian.

24.2 🔊
1. Janine could dance very well.
2. Janine could dance beautifully.
3. Janine could speak five languages very well.
4. Janine could speak five languages beautifully.
5. Janine could play the piano very well.
6. Janine could play the piano beautifully.
7. You could dance very well.
8. You could dance beautifully.
9. You could speak five languages very well.
10. You could speak five languages beautifully.
11. You could play the piano very well.
12. You could play the piano beautifully.
13. Yanis could dance very well.
14. Yanis could dance beautifully.
15. Yanis could speak five languages very well.
16. Yanis could speak five languages beautifully.
17. Yanis could play the piano very well.
18. Yanis could play the piano beautifully.

24.3
1 eight.
2 12 years old.
3 six languages.
4 bake cakes.
5 climb a tree.

24.4 🔊
1 Greg could swim when he was four.
2 Simon couldn't come to the party.
3 Jean could speak Japanese.
4 My dog could run very quickly.
5 Greg could speak fluent Russian.
6 I couldn't drive because of the snow.
7 We couldn't find your street.

25

25.1 🔊
1 science fiction
2 crime
3 newspaper
4 main character
5 horror
6 exhibition
7 author
8 bookstore
9 audience
10 TV show
11 villain
12 clap
13 hero
14 action
15 novel
16 thriller
17 director
18 movie
19 musical
20 comedy
21 documentary
22 romance
23 play

26

26.1 🔊
1 made
2 sang
3 put
4 began
5 met
6 sold
7 took
8 ate
9 saw
10 slept
11 bought

26.2 🔊
1 Sophie **took** her cat to the vet.
2 I **wrote** a letter. Did you get it?
3 We **met** some interesting people today.
4 Roger **bought** a new car on Wednesday.
5 Jane **saw** a really good film yesterday.
6 I **got** a postcard from my brother.
7 Derek **went** home at 11pm.
8 Archie **made** a cake for my birthday.
9 My son **began** school yesterday.
10 I **found** my glasses under the bed.
11 Sid **felt** happy when he finished school.
12 Bobby **sang** a song to his mother.

26.3 🔊
1 Samantha and Cathy **ate** pizza after work.
2 Katy **went** to the disco with Ben on Friday night.
3 Miguel **wrote** a beautiful song about his wife Christine.
4 Pauline and Emma **got** lots of presents for Christmas this year.
5 The kids **saw** a play at the theater with us last week.
6 Keith **bought** a new guitar for his brother Patrick on his birthday.
7 Emily **slept** in a tent in the back yard last night.
8 Pablo **sang** a traditional song at Elma and Mark's wedding.
9 Tammy **sold** her old computer to her neighbor Anna.
10 They **felt** sad after watching the film about a boy who lost his dog.
11 Mick **began** to read a new book yesterday evening.
12 Joan **found** a gold necklace in the garden while she was gardening.
13 We **took** the children to the movie theater next to the shopping mall.
14 Warren **made** a delicious sandwich for his daughter's lunch.

26.4 🔊
1 **First**, Bob ate some soup. Then he had a burger and a sandwich.
2 My cousins have stayed for six weeks! They've **finally** decided to go home.
3 First, I went to the baker's. **Next**, I went to the butcher's next door.
4 Samantha gave me a letter. **After that**, she left to go back home.

26.5 🔊
1 Did Samantha take her money? **No, she left it on the table.**
2 Did you get some bread? **Sorry, the baker was closed.**
3 Did you meet Rebecca's boyfriend? **Yes, he's really handsome.**
4 Did you find your glasses? **Yes, they were in the bathroom.**
5 Did you see any tigers? **No, the zoo was closed.**
6 Did Dan buy a new car? **No, it was too expensive.**
7 Did you go to the movies? **No, there were no good movies on.**

8 Did Jim make that cake? **No, he bought it at the baker's.**

9 Did Billy eat his dinner? **Yes, he ate everything.**

10 Did you write him a letter? **No, I sent him a text.**

11 Did you sell your house? **Yes, we're moving on Saturday.**

12 Did you begin your course? **No, it starts on Wednesday.**

13 Did you sleep well? **No, it was too noisy in my room.**

26.6 🔊

1 What **did you see at the movie theater?**

2 Who **did Sarah take to the party?**

3 What **did you have for dinner on Friday?**

4 Where **did they go on vacation?**

5 What **did Steve buy?**

6 What **did Jim eat for lunch?**

7 Who **did Kelly meet last week?**

8 Where **did Peter put his phone?**

9 Where **did you find my watch?**

10 What **did Anna make for lunch?**

11 What **did you get from Doug?**

12 What **did Peter sing for Elma?**

13 When **did your sister come to see you?**

26.7
ACROSS
1 saw **2** sold **3** felt **4** bought
DOWN
5 made **6** took **7** slept

27

27.1 🔊
1 nail
2 bolt
3 jigsaw
4 tape measure
5 nut
6 hammer
7 screw
8 rake
9 clamp
10 screwdriver
11 trowel
12 pliers
13 fork
14 saw
15 drill

27.2 🔊
1 cutting board (US) / chopping board (UK)
2 peeler
3 spatula
4 grater
5 ladle
6 kitchen knife
7 corkscrew
8 whisk
9 scissors
10 can opener
11 wooden spoon

28

28.1
POSITIVE OPINIONS
1 funny **2** thrilling **3** exciting
NEGATIVE OPINIONS
4 boring **5** slow **6** silly **7** confusing

28.2 🔊
1 It's a movie about a racing car driver.
2 It's a movie about two brothers.
3 It's a book about two young sisters from the country.
4 It's a story about London in the 1890s.
5 It's a musical about a couple who got married.

28.3
1 The first bank is in Munich.
2 They turn off the alarms.
3 The thieves are caught on video surveillance camera.
4 The thieves go to prison after they are caught.
5 The reviewer thinks it is a bit slow and not very well acted.
6 It is based on the Shakespeare play *Macbeth*.
7 Macbeth meets three witches.
8 King Duncan gives Macbeth the title of Thane of Cawdor.
9 Macbeth plots with his wife.
10 Macbeth kills King Duncan.
11 The reviewer thinks it is thrilling.

28.4
A 6
B 4
C 1
D 5
E 2
F 3

28.5 🔊
1 Jo **didn't enjoy** the show because it was boring.
2 Hannah **liked** the film because it was fun.
3 I **hated** the musical because the story was silly.
4 He enjoyed the play because it was **thrilling**.
5 I **didn't like** the play because it was boring.
6 Paul hated the show because it was **scary**.
7 I **hated** the show because it was slow.
8 She liked the story because it was **romantic**.
9 He **enjoyed** the movie because it was exciting.
10 I hated the play because it was **boring**.
11 He **didn't enjoy** the film because it was scary.
12 She liked the book because it was **exciting**.
13 I **didn't like** the play because it was silly.
14 The movie was **thrilling** and they loved it.
15 I **enjoyed** the musical because it was romantic.

28.6 🔊
1 I hated the musical because it was silly.
2 Anna loved the film because it was thrilling.
3 Tom didn't enjoy the movie because it was slow.
4 Sam enjoyed the film because it was funny.
5 Kay loved the book because it had a romantic ending.
6 Jim hated the show because it was boring.
7 I really liked the play because it was thrilling.
8 I didn't like the book because it was scary.
9 I didn't enjoy the opera because it was difficult to understand.
10 They enjoyed the book because it had an exciting story.

29

29.1 🔊
1 Did you take many photographs?

2 Did Jim have a good vacation?
3 Did Fred take a taxi to the airport?
4 Did you stay in a nice hotel?
5 Did you visit the Eiffel Tower?

29.2 🔊

1 Did they see any crocodiles?
2 Did you eat any Indian food?
3 Did Paul sail to Corfu?
4 Did my sister go skiing in the Alps?
5 Did Chris stay in a cheap hotel?
6 Did your mom go waterskiing?
7 Did you visit any beautiful beaches?
8 Did you buy any presents for the kids?
9 Did Bob and Sally have pizza for lunch?

29.3

1 Did
2 Didn't
3 Did
4 Did
5 Didn't

29.4

1 Yes, he did.
2 Yes, it did.
3 No, he didn't.
4 Yes, he did.
5 Yes, he did.
6 Yes, they did.
7 Yes, she did.
8 No, he didn't.
9 No, he didn't.

29.5 🔊

1 Who did you stay with? **With Marco's cousins.**
2 What did you visit while you were there? **The Tower of Pisa.**
3 What time did you arrive at the airport? **At 11pm.**
4 How did you get there? **We took the bus.**
5 When did you come back? **On Wednesday evening.**
6 What did you eat there? **Some wonderful fish.**

29.6

1 Thursday
2 A T-shirt
3 By boat
4 Fish and chips

29.7 🔊

1 When did you visit Hong Kong?
2 Who did you travel with?
3 What did you eat in the evening?
4 What did you buy there?
5 How did you get to the airport?
6 What did you visit in Rome?
7 What did you do in Las Vegas?

29.8 🔊

1 Where **did you go** on vacation?
2 When **did you arrive** at the hotel?
3 Who **did you go** on vacation with?
4 How **did you get** to the airport?
5 Why **did you go** to Sardinia?
6 What **did you eat** at the restaurant?
7 What **did you do** in Mallorca?

30

30.1

1 False **2** False **3** True
4 False **5** True

30.2

A 2
B 4
C 1
D 6
E 8
F 7
G 5
H 3

30.3

1 He **has been** an English teacher for two years.
2 He **studied** English in college.
3 While **he was** a student, he worked in a bar.
4 He **really liked** working with others.
5 Gary **taught** English at St. Mark's School.
6 He **is now working** at BKS Language Services.
7 He **teaches** adults English now.
8 He **loves playing** soccer in his free time.
9 He also **loves** walking in the mountains.

30.4 🔊

1 What **did you do** at your last job at the restaurant?
2 When **can you start** working for our college?

3 Why **do you want** to work for our company?
4 Where **do you see** yourself in five years' time?
5 **Do you like** working with other people?
6 Why **did you leave** your last job as a receptionist?

31

31.1 🔊

1 What **did you eat?**
2 Who **did you go to the new café with?**
3 What **did you see last week?**
4 Who **did Anna call yesterday?**
5 Who **did you visit on Wednesday?**
6 What **does David want?**
7 What **does Fiona like having?**
8 Who **did you see this morning?**
9 What **does Tina enjoy doing?**

31.2 🔊

1. Who did you call yesterday?
2. Who did you call on Tuesday?
3. Who did she call yesterday?
4. Who did she call on Tuesday?
5. Who did they call yesterday?
6. Who did they call on Tuesday?
7. Who did you meet yesterday?
8. Who did you meet on Tuesday?
9. Who did she meet yesterday?
10. Who did she meet on Tuesday?
11. Who did they meet yesterday?
12. Who did they meet on Tuesday?
13. What did you do yesterday?
14. What did you do on Tuesday?
15. What did she do yesterday?
16. What did she do on Tuesday?
17. What did they do yesterday?
18. What did they do on Tuesday?

31.3 🔊

1 Who called the bank yesterday?
2 What did the new customer order?
3 Who gave the staff a raise?
4 Who did you see at the meeting?
5 What does the manager want?
6 Who wants a higher salary?
7 What did the boss say to you?
8 Who did you call on Monday?
9 What time did the meeting start?

31.4 🔊
1 Who **emailed the prices to the customer?**
2 Who **started a full-time job last month?**
3 Who **doesn't want a nine-to-five job?**
4 Who **gave a presentation about sales?**
5 Who **had a good meeting yesterday?**
6 Who **didn't come to the meeting this morning?**
7 Who **started work at 7am today?**
8 Who **won the prize for Manager of the Month?**
9 What **is big enough for the staff?**
10 Who **wants to work for your company?**
11 What **was great this year?**
12 Who **wants a discount?**

31.5 🔊
1 **Who** asked for a higher salary?
2 **What** did Phil give the staff?
3 **Who** gave a presentation?
4 **What** did she cook today?
5 **What** kind of job do you have?
6 **Who** started a new job today?
7 **What** did you buy for Carla?
8 **Who** didn't hit his sales targets?
9 **Who** does she work for?
10 **Who** sent the boss an email?
11 **What** did they say yesterday?
12 **Who** did she meet on Tuesday?
13 **What** did you tell Amanda?
14 **Who** asked for a discount?
15 **Who** spoke to the customer?
16 **What** kind of music do you like?
17 **Who** has a part-time job?
18 **Who** gave the staff a day off?
19 **What** did Dan send the boss?

31.6
1 his boss
2 yes
3 both of them
4 the US
5 IT software
6 the UK
7 £300
8 a promotion
9 her boss

31.7 🔊
1 Who wrote to the customers?
2 Who met their sales targets this month?
3 What did the customer ask for?
4 Who gave a presentation?

5 What did the manager give the staff?
6 Who called the new customers?
7 What did the new customer order?
8 What job did Sandra start last week?
9 What time did the meeting start?
10 Who took notes at the meeting?
11 What did the area manager want?
12 Who wants a higher salary?
13 What did the boss say to you yesterday?
14 Who called you on Monday?
15 Who gave you the notes from the meeting?
16 What kind of job does Karen have?
17 Who did you see at the meeting?

31.8 🔊
1. Who read the letter?
2. Who called the customer?
3. Who called the boss?
4. Who saw the letter?
5. Who saw the customer?
6. Who saw the boss?

32

32.1 🔊
1 There's **someone** at the door. Perhaps it's the new neighbor.
2 My cousin wants **someone** to go on vacation with him to Argentina.
3 I need **someone** to help me with my homework. It's very difficult.
4 Does **anyone** know John's phone number so I can give it to Sue?
5 I met **someone** interesting on vacation and we went to the beach together.
6 There's **someone** in the museum who you can ask for directions.
7 Is **anyone** going to see the movie tonight with Rachel and Monica?
8 **Someone** left an umbrella in the office on Monday.
9 I need **someone** to go to the party with me tonight.
10 Does **anyone** want to go for coffee later in the café?
11 **Someone** knocked on the door this morning when I was in the kitchen.

32.2
1 everyone
2 no one
3 everyone
4 someone
5 no one
6 everyone
7 someone
8 everyone

32.3 🔊
1 I didn't give **anybody** your phone number.
2 Is **anybody** coming for lunch with me?
3 Nobody **likes** my new green shirt.
4 No one **is** coming to the movies tonight.
5 **Nobody** remembered Ben's birthday. Poor Ben!
6 Everyone **is** coming to my party tonight.
7 Does **anybody** need help with the exercise?

32.4 🔊
1. Everybody went to the restaurant last night.
2. Everybody asked about the new job.
3. Everybody wants to go to a party with me tonight.
4. Someone went to the restaurant last night.
5. Someone asked about the new job.
6. Someone wants to go to a party with me tonight.
7. Nobody went to the restaurant last night.
8. Nobody asked about the new job.
9. Nobody wants to go to a party with me tonight.

33

33.1 🔊
1 Were you?
2 They didn't?
3 She wasn't?
4 Did she?
5 Did you?

33.2 🔊
1 We gave Charlotte a dress for her birthday. **Did you?**
2 Our dog likes to sleep under the bed. **Does it?**
3 Miguel isn't from Spain. **Isn't he?**

4 I wasn't impressed with the new film.
Weren't you?
5 Frank wasn't at the meeting on Thursday.
He wasn't?
6 My parents don't like watching TV.
They don't?
7 I like your new glasses. **Do you?**
8 Cynthia didn't call me again.
Didn't she?
9 Paul didn't go to the party last night.
He didn't?
10 Chris and Dan went to the Costa del Sol.
Did they?

33.3 🔊
1 **Does** she?
2 He **did**?
3 **Does** he?
4 You **don't**?
5 They **do**?
6 **Isn't** she?
7 **Wasn't** she?

33.4 🔊
1 **Did** you?
2 He **was**?
3 **Didn't** you?
4 **Did** they?
5 **Was** it?
6 You **did**?
7 It **does**?
8 **Did** you?
9 **Did** he?

34

34.1 🔊
1 musician
2 fun fair
3 applause
4 bar
5 go dancing
6 concert
7 menu
8 concert hall
9 meet friends
10 buy a ticket
11 book club
12 art gallery
13 waitress
14 waiter
15 go bowling

16 go to the movies
17 audience
18 do karaoke
19 circus
20 band
21 orchestra
22 night club
23 restaurant
24 opera
25 ballet
26 go to a party
27 see a play

35

35.1 🔊
1 We **are going** sailing in the Mediterranean this summer.
2 Shelley **is traveling** around India in July next year.
3 We **are playing** baseball with our friends after school.
4 I **am watching** a movie at the theater with my boyfriend tonight.

35.2
1 future
2 present
3 present
4 future

35.3 🔊
1 We're going to France **in** June.
2 I'm playing tennis **on** Wednesday.
3 My grandmother was born **in** 1944.
4 Christmas Day is **on** December 25.
5 I'm finishing work **in** 2025.
6 I bought a new car **on** Wednesday.
7 New Year's Day is **on** January 1.
8 Pete was born **in** 1990.
9 I saw my friend Clive **on** Saturday.
10 Derek starts his job **on** Tuesday.
11 Alexander's exam is **on** June 4.
12 We finish school **in** July.
13 I'm going to the theater **on** Friday evening.

35.4 🔊
1 I'd love to, but I can't. I **am studying** for my exam.
2 That would be nice, but I **am meeting** my girlfriend in town.

3 Oh, I'd love to, but I **am going** on vacation to Spain.
4 I'd like to, but I can't. I **am having** lunch with Sue today.

35.5
1 True **2** False **3** True
4 False **5** False

35.6
1 I'm sorry, but I'm going to the theater that evening.
2 Sorry, I can't. I'm going to see a band.
3 Sorry, I can't. I'm having lunch with Irene.
4 That sounds nice, but I'm going on vacation to Mexico.
5 I'd love to, but I'm playing soccer with my colleagues.
6 Sorry, I can't. I'm studying for my exams then.
7 That sounds nice, but I'm going shopping with Tom.
8 I'd like to, but I'm going to dinner with Carl that night.
9 I'd love to, but I'm meeting my sister that day.

35.7 🔊
1 That'd be fun, but **I'm going ice skating with Victoria**.
2 I'd like to, but **I'm going swimming**.
3 That sounds nice, but **I'm visiting old friends from school**.
4 That would be fun, but **I'm going to Sam's party**.
5 Sorry, I can't. **I'm visiting my grandparents**.
6 That sounds nice, but **I'm studying for the math exam**.
7 I can't. **I'm going shopping for groceries**.

36

36.1
1 True **2** False **3** True **4** False
5 False **6** False

36.2 🔊
1 Angela **is** going to clean her bedroom.
2 Will **is** not going to buy a new car.
3 They **are** going to stay in a hotel.

4 Mary and George **are** going to visit Egypt.

5 Shane **is** going to study IT in college.

6 You **are** going to visit your grandmother.

7 Liv **is** going to finish her work later.

8 Aziz **is** going to travel to Rome this fall.

9 They **are** not going to play soccer today.

10 I **am** going to cook steak tonight.

11 We **are** going to eat pizza for dinner.

12 Murat **is** going to listen to the radio.

13 I **am** not going to eat frogs' legs again.

36.3 🔊

1 Tim is going to eat pizza tonight.

2 Ann is not going to drive to Utah.

3 We are going to visit Boston this fall.

4 Fred is not going to study German.

5 They are going to buy a puppy.

6 I am going to travel this summer.

7 We are going to play soccer.

8 I'm going to start an English course.

9 Angela is going to clean her room.

10 I am going to study at the library.

11 They are going to sell their house.

36.4 🔊

1 We **are going to cook** a chicken tonight.

2 Sharon and Flo **are not going to play** tennis this weekend.

3 I **am going to visit** my aunt in France in September.

4 Pedro **is going to learn** a musical instrument at school.

36.5 🔊

1 Cynthia is going to walk her dog.

2 Phil is going to take a photo.

3 Sharon is going to bake a cake.

4 Janet is going to visit Hawaii.

5 Mike is going to watch a movie.

36.6 🔊

1 I **am going to visit** Berlin next week.

2 Rachel **is going to paint** her kitchen on the weekend.

3 My sister **is going to study** French in college.

4 Stuart and Colin **are going to climb** that mountain.

5 Patrick **is not going to drive** to work today.

6 Angus **is going to live** in Edinburgh.

7 We **are going to buy** a new house.

8 Samantha **is going to watch** a movie tonight.

9 Helen **is going to start** her new job next week.

36.7 🔊

1 Jessica is not going to study **physics in college.**

2 We are going to paint **the kitchen a different color.**

3 Jenny is going to go **on vacation in the Bahamas.**

4 Theo is going to wear a suit **for his job interview.**

5 My uncle is not going to eat **a hamburger for lunch.**

6 Olivia is going to ride **her horse this weekend.**

7 I am going to bake **a cake for Christmas.**

36.8

Ⓐ 6

Ⓑ 5

Ⓒ 4

Ⓓ 2

Ⓔ 1

Ⓕ 3

37

37.1 🔊

1 The boy is going to **fall off** the wall.

2 It looks like it's going to **rain** soon.

3 It's 8:29pm. We're going to **miss** the train.

4 Oh dear! I think they're going to **crash.**

5 I think she's going to **buy** that coat.

37.2 🔊

1 Oh no, it's started to rain cats and dogs. We are going to get wet!

2 That girl has been teasing the dog all day. I think it is going to bite her.

3 Hurry up! The train leaves in five minutes and you are going to miss it.

4 That's Claire's purse. She's going to leave for college in a minute.

5 It looks like he is going to win this race. He's a long way in front.

6 The team captain has a microphone. Do you think he's going to sing the national anthem?

7 The weather forecast says it is not going to rain at all next week.

8 This traffic jam is enormous. I am going to be late for work again.

9 That dog is trying to open your shopping bag. I think he's going to steal your food.

10 Raymond is going to study science in college.

11 Shelley is not going to win the competition. The other players are all too good.

12 They're not very good at skating. It looks like they are going to fall over.

37.3 🔊

1 Kelly is going to pass her English exam.

2 We are not going to catch our train.

3 John is going to ask Amy to marry him.

4 Danny is going to win this race.

37.4 🔊

1 Tamara is not well today. **She isn't going to come to work.**

2 Look at that small child on the wall! **She's going to fall off!**

3 Jim's working so hard this year. **I think he's going to pass his exam.**

4 The trains aren't working today. **We're going to be late for work.**

5 Look at those awful black clouds. **I think it's going to rain later.**

6 I bought pasta this morning. **I'm going to make spaghetti bolognese.**

7 Mia is buying milk. **She is going to make ice cream.**

37.5 🔊

1 Sharon **is going to eat** a piece of cake.

2 Take an umbrella. It **is going to rain** later.

3 The children **are going to enjoy** the movie tonight.

4 My husband **is going to be** late for work.

5 Mrs. O'Connell **is going to play** the piano in a minute.

6 Be careful! You **are going to drop** the vase.

7 Bill and Claire **are going to bake** a birthday cake for Paul.

37.6 🔊

1. I am going to be late for work.

2. I am going to pass the exam.

3. I am going to miss the bus.

4. I am not going to be late for work.

5. I am not going to pass the exam.

6. I am not going to miss the bus.
7. Dan is going to be late for work.
8. Dan is going to pass the exam.
9. Dan is going to miss the bus.
10. Dan is not going to be late for work.
11. Dan is not going to pass the exam.
12. Dan is not going to miss the bus.
13. We are going to be late for work.
14. We are going to pass the exam.
15. We are going to miss the bus.
16. We are not going to be late for work.
17. We are not going to pass the exam.
18. We are not going to miss the bus.

38

38.1 🔊
1. tiger
2. turtle
3. crab
4. fly
5. whale
6. buffalo
7. mouse
8. butterfly
9. cow
10. giraffe
11. shark
12. bear
13. spider
14. kangaroo
15. dolphin
16. lizard
17. fish
18. bull
19. monkey
20. insect
21. snake
22. octopus
23. bird
24. rhino
25. bee
26. elephant
27. camel
28. crocodile
29. frog
30. rat
31. lion

39

39.1 🔊
1. Ronaldo **won't go** to bed before midnight.
2. The kids **will have** a great time in Florida next summer.
3. You **will love** the new coat I just bought for the winter.
4. Mia **won't eat** anything with meat in it.
5. My sister **will be** late for school again.
6. Eric **will want** to eat steak and fries for his dinner.
7. Noah **will win** the 400m race at the track competition.
8. My children **won't like** that flavor of ice cream.
9. Charlotte **will marry** her boyfriend this year.
10. I **will stay** at home and watch TV tonight.
11. Arnie **will go** swimming with Bob and Sue.

39.2 🔊
1. Chris **won't** go on vacation this year.
2. **I'll** write you a postcard from Ibiza.
3. **They'll** visit their grandmother next week.
4. Ethan **won't** go to summer camp this year.
5. Isla **won't** reply to my messages.
6. **We'll** visit you when we are in San Diego.
7. I **won't** be at the party this evening.
8. Eleanor **won't** make dinner for us tonight.
9. **I'll** take the children to the movie theater tonight.
10. Fred **won't** be at the party tomorrow.

39.3
1. He'll bring some chicken.
2. She'll make some sandwiches.
3. She'll get some juice.
4. They'll make a cake.
5. It'll be nice and sunny.

39.4 🔊
1. I think I'll visit Rome next year.
2. I don't think Bob will be at the party.
3. I think we'll go to a restaurant tonight.
4. I think my brother will visit us this year.
5. I don't think the kids will go to school tomorrow.
6. I don't think it'll be sunny tomorrow.
7. I think we'll win the lottery this week.
8. I think Simone will want to go to the theater.
9. I don't think it'll snow this winter.

39.5 🔊
1. Look at those clouds. It **is going to** rain.
2. You **won't** like this movie.
3. There's so much traffic! We **are going to** be late.
4. Bob never does his homework. He **is going to** fail the exam.
5. **Will he** come to the party tomorrow?
6. Jenny practices the guitar every day. She **is going to** be a great musician.
7. Bob looks tired. He **isn't going to** finish the race.
8. I think Chloe **is going to** win the competition. I love her voice.
9. Peter **is going to** fall asleep. He looks tired.
10. It **will be** a delicious meal.

39.6
1. Alice thinks the movie is going to be very exciting.
2. The tickets will all be sold.
3. She doesn't think Stu will enjoy the film.
4. Alice is going to get the bus.
5. Alice will buy Suki a coffee.
6. Alice thinks the day will be fun.

40

40.1 🔊
1. There's no milk, so I **won't have** tea. I **will have** black coffee.
2. The 11:05 train is late, so we **won't get** that one. We **will take** the bus.
3. I don't feel well. I **won't go** to work. I **will call** my boss and tell him.
4. I left work late yesterday. I **won't stay** late today. I **will leave** at 5pm.
5. I'm tired. I **won't make** dinner. I **will ask** my partner to make it.
6. There are no buses and it's raining. I **won't walk**. I **will get** a taxi home.
7. It is snowing. I **won't drive** to work. I **will get** the bus today.
8. It's late. I **won't walk** the dog in the park. I **will walk** up the road instead.

9 It's sunny. I **won't take** an umbrella. I **will wear** my sun hat.

10 There's a lot of traffic. I **won't drive**. I **will walk** there.

11 I **won't take** my books back to the library. I **will do** it tomorrow.

40.2
1 Won't do
2 Will do
3 Won't do
4 Will do
5 Will do

40.3 ◄))
1 It's going to rain, so **I'll take an umbrella with me.**
2 It's my sister's birthday today, so **I'll make her a cake.**
3 I forgot my sandwich, so **I'll buy one from the deli.**
4 I like those jeans, so **I'll buy them.**
5 It's dark, so **I won't walk home through the park.**
6 It's a long train trip, so **I'll take a book with me.**
7 There's nothing to eat, so **I'll get a takeout pizza.**

40.4 ◄))
1 In that case, I'll **take** my umbrella.
2 In that case, I'll **stay** at home.
3 In that case, I'll **have** rice.
4 In that case, I'll **call** you later.
5 In that case, I'll **give** you a ride.

40.5 ◄))
1 I think I'll have the fish.
2 I think I'll stay in tonight.
3 I think I'll watch the news.
4 I think I'll take my raincoat.
5 I think I'll call Simon.
6 I think I'll leave work early.
7 I think I'll ask Jenny to make dinner.

40.6
1 True **2** False **3** False **4** True
5 False **6** False **7** True

40.7 ◄))
1. I think he'll win the race.
2. I will win the race.
3. I won't win the race.
4. I think he'll go to bed soon.

5. I will go to bed soon.
6. I won't go to bed soon.
7. He will win the race.
8. He won't win the race.
9. He will go to bed soon.
10. He won't go to bed soon.

41

41.1 ◄))
1 Paul might not come to Jane's party.
2 I will go on vacation with my sister.
3 Emma might visit her grandmother this weekend.
4 I won't be at work tomorrow.
5 Jim won't do a bungee jump.
6 Sam won't go to Spain this summer.
7 Tina might be able to give you a ride home.

41.2
1 I won't go to the movies tonight.
   I will go to the movies tonight.
2 We might go to Dan's party.
   We will go to Dan's party.
3 I won't go to the bank at lunchtime.
   I might go to the bank at lunchtime.
4 I won't buy a newspaper.
   I will buy a newspaper.
5 You might work late tonight.
   You will work late tonight.
6 Karen won't move next month.
   Karen might move next month.

41.3
1 I will
2 it will
3 I won't
4 I will
5 I might
6 I won't
7 I will
8 I might
9 It will
10 I might
11 Will you

41.4 ◄))
1 Will you buy a new computer? **I don't know, they're very expensive.**
2 Where will you meet Anna? **I'll meet her at the train station.**

3 Will you go to John's party? **I don't know. I'm pretty tired.**
4 How will you get to the station? **I think Sean will give me a ride.**
5 What will you do this afternoon? **I don't know. I might watch a movie.**
6 When will you get your exam results? **I'm not sure. Perhaps next Monday.**
7 Who will you see at the party? **I don't know. I might see Katie.**
8 Will you make dinner tonight? **I don't know. I think Diana will make it.**
9 Where will you go on vacation this year? **I'm not sure. I think I'll go to France.**
10 What will you buy at the mall? **I don't know. I might buy some new shoes.**

41.5
1 Yes, she will.
2 He might.
3 No, she won't.
4 Yes, he will.
5 She might.

41.6 ◄))
1 Adam **will** ride a bike.
   Adam **might** watch a film.
   Adam **won't** cook dinner.
2 Leanne **will** go running.
   Leanne **might** play tennis.
   Leanne **won't** go to bed early.
3 Peter **will** drive his car.
   Peter **might** walk home.
   Peter **won't** ride a motorcycle.
4 Carla **will** go to the hairdresser.
   Carla **might** go to the supermarket.
   Carla **won't** go swimming.
5 Ken **will** have coffee.
   Ken **might** read a newspaper.
   Ken **won't** eat a burger.

42

42.1 ◄))
1 It's dark and cold outside. You **shouldn't** walk home.
2 Tim's driving later. He **shouldn't** drink that wine.
3 Clara is very tired. She **should** go to bed early tonight.
4 It's very cold here. You **should** wear a sweater.

5 Flora feels ill. She **should** go to the doctor tomorrow.

42.2 🔊
1 Carla should take time off this year.
2 Casey shouldn't buy herself a dog.
3 Kevin should save some money for his vacation.
4 Rahul should visit his mother more often.
5 Sherry shouldn't eat cheese late at night.

42.3
1 Kevin should go out with Sandra.
2 Paul should wear a hat.
3 Gabby should start a diet.
4 Barry should buy a tie for his grandfather.
5 Murat should wear a suit for work.
6 Phillip should do a language course.
7 Nicky should get a pet.

42.4 🔊
1 I have no money. **You should find a better paid job.**
2 I don't speak English well. **You should do a language course.**
3 I can't find a boyfriend. **You should go get some coffee with my brother.**
4 I don't have any nice clothes. **You should go shopping with me next week.**
5 I don't have many friends. **You should join some clubs to meet people.**
6 I want to lose some weight. **You should go jogging every evening.**
7 I can't sleep at night. **You should do something relaxing before bed.**
8 I can't wake up in the morning. **You should buy an alarm clock.**
9 I want to speak perfect French. **You should live in France for a year.**
10 I want to do well in my exams. **You should work hard at school.**
11 I'm feeling very stressed. **You should take a vacation.**

43

43.1 🔊
1 I haven't bought my friend a present. **You could go to the store on Park Street.**
2 I didn't pass my English exam. **You could take it again in June.**

3 I left my phone at your house. **We could go back and get it.**
4 I'm feeling really hungry. **We could get a hamburger for lunch.**
5 I lost my job at the supermarket. **You could work at the new café.**

43.2 🔊
1 My house is too small for my family. You **could buy** a bigger house.
2 Jamal wants to speak better English. He **could practice** every day.
3 I don't know what to do when I finish school. You **could apply** to a college.
4 They don't have jobs right now. They **could look** online for a new one.
5 My sister doesn't like taking the bus. She **could learn** to drive herself.

43.3
1 practice at home; take lessons with a teacher
2 travel to Peru; visit Buenos Aires
3 cook some pasta; buy some fish
4 buy her some perfume; get her chocolates

43.4 🔊
1 You could **buy a new one**.
2 You could **go on a blind date**.
3 You could **buy an alarm clock**.
4 You could **take it again**.

44

44.1 🔊
1 clear the table
2 mend the fence
3 sweep the floor
4 wash the car
5 buy groceries
6 fold clothes
7 walk the dog
8 clean the windows
9 do the ironing
10 dry the dishes
11 set the table
12 scrub the floor
13 do the gardening
14 chop vegetables
15 paint a room
16 mop the floor
17 change the sheets

18 feed the pets
19 do the laundry
20 hang a picture
21 cook dinner
22 vacuum the carpet
23 load the dishwasher
24 water the plants
25 dust
26 tidy
27 mow the lawn

45

45.1
1 started
2 closed
3 tidied
4 cleaned
5 washed
6 painted
7 cooked

45.2 🔊
1 Sharon **has mowed** the lawn.
2 You **haven't dusted** the living room.
3 Mike **has painted** the walls.
4 Mom **has sailed** to France and Italy.
5 I **have mopped** the kitchen floor.
6 He **hasn't cooked** the dinner.
7 They **have called** the police.
8 We **have washed** the car.
9 Jim **has changed** the sheets.
10 She **hasn't tidied** her room.
11 Karen **has visited** Peru.

45.3 🔊
1 Has Charlene mopped the floor?
2 Has Sue changed her sheets?
3 Have you cleaned the windows?
4 Has Hank tidied his bedroom?
5 Has Janine cooked dinner?
6 Has Mrs. Underwood visited Ireland?
7 Have you started college?
8 Has Sid walked to school?
9 Has she called her grandmother?
10 Have you watched this film?
11 Has Adam painted his bedroom?

45.4 🔊
1 Katy **hasn't** cleaned the bathroom.
2 We **haven't** left school.
3 I **haven't** tidied the kitchen.

4 My mom **hasn't** read the letter.

5 We **haven't** painted the backyard fence.

6 James **hasn't** tidied his bedroom.

7 You **haven't** cooked the dinner.

8 Terry **hasn't** visited the US.

9 Anne **hasn't** been to London.

45.5 🔊

1 Peter **has won** the race.

2 We **have eaten** all the pastries.

3 Michelle **has started** a new job.

4 We **have finished** our chores.

5 Dave **has kept** a seat for you.

6 I **have spent** all my money.

7 Chan **has broken** the window.

8 They **have given** Grandpa new slippers.

9 Jacob **has heard** the bad news.

10 Mr. Evans **has left** the building.

11 Mike **has put** the cup away.

12 He **has told** me about life in the 1960s.

13 Antoine **has taught** me French.

14 Craig **has written** a novel.

15 Doug **has seen** that movie twice.

16 We **have been** in France for three weeks.

17 Abe **has flown** to Paris for the weekend.

18 You **have forgotten** my birthday again!

19 I **have found** a new job.

20 Zac **has done** his homework.

21 Hugh **has driven** to work today.

22 She **has taken** her son to school.

23 Owen **has bought** a new shirt.

45.6

1 No, he hasn't.

2 No, they haven't.

3 Yes, he has.

4 No, she hasn't.

5 Yes, she has.

6 No, he hasn't.

7 No, he hasn't.

45.7 🔊

1 They **have told** me the news.

2 You **have forgotten** my name again!

3 Sim **has heard** the news.

4 Derek **has bought** a new tie.

5 John **has done** his homework.

6 We **have seen** that movie twice.

7 Jenny **has eaten** her dinner.

8 Amy **has given** me a nice present.

9 I **have put** my shirt in the closet.

10 He **has found** his watch under the bed.

11 The children **have broken** the window.

12 They **have watched** the soccer game.

13 Jo **has driven** the car.

14 Tom **has washed** the dishes.

15 He **has left** his wallet at the store.

45.8 🔊

1. Pete has mopped the floor.

2. Pete hasn't mopped the floor.

3. Pete has cleaned the bathroom.

4. Pete hasn't cleaned the bathroom.

5. Clare has mopped the floor.

6. Clare hasn't mopped the floor.

7. Clare has cleaned the bathroom.

8. Clare hasn't cleaned the bathroom.

9. You have mopped the floor.

10. You haven't mopped the floor.

11. You have cleaned the bathroom.

12. You haven't cleaned the bathroom.

46

46.1 🔊

1 **Did you go** to work yesterday? There was an important meeting at 11 am.

2 Mom **made** a birthday cake for Samantha last weekend. It was delicious.

3 Owen went to Spain last month. He **sent** us a postcard of Madrid.

4 I love the film *Trip to Heaven*. I **have seen** it five times.

5 Deena **has visited** both the Grand Canyon and Monument Valley in Arizona.

46.2 🔊

1 Yes, **I've been surfing** many times.

2 Yes, **I went** there in 2014.

3 Yes, my dad **has been** twice.

4 No, **I've never seen** it.

5 Yes, **he did a bungee jump** last year.

46.3 🔊

1 Fran has been to France many times. She **visited** France last summer.

2 David went rock-climbing in 2013 and 2014. He **has been** rock-climbing twice.

3 Cam went bungee-jumping last summer. She **has been** bungee-jumping once.

4 Jamie goes surfing most weekends. He **went** surfing yesterday.

5 Rachel climbed Mount Fuji in 2013 and 2014. She **has climbed** it twice.

6 Jim went diving in Egypt last summer and spring. He **has been** diving there twice.

7 I went wing-walking in New Zealand last year. It **was** amazing!

8 My brother went paragliding last summer. He **has been** paragliding once.

9 Archie goes snowboarding every winter. He **has been** snowboarding eight times.

10 My cousin goes caving most weekends. I **have never been** caving.

11 Ray goes windsurfing most weekends. He **has gone** windsurfing today.

12 My brother loves racing. He **has raced** in many competitions.

13 I have skied in Austria three times. I **went** skiing there last winter.

14 Tom loves kitesurfing. He **has been** kitesurfing in many different countries.

46.4

PRESENT PERFECT

1 have been

2 have had

3 have visited

4 has been

PAST SIMPLE

5 visited

6 went

7 ate

8 was

46.5 🔊

1 I love Florence. I've **been** there three times.

2 Tina has **gone** to Spain. She'll be back in two weeks.

3 Have you ever **been** skiing in Norway?

4 I've **been** to the new museum in town. It's very crowded.

5 John and Kate have **gone** to the theater. They're meeting you there.

6 I have **gone** to Hero's to meet some friends. See you there later.

46.6

1 True 2 False 3 Not Given 4 True

5 True 6 False 7 False

46.7 🔊

1 Larry and Michel **went** to the US twice in 2014.

2 Hannah **has dived** in Australia many times.

3 Jim and Rose **made** a cake last weekend.

4 Debbie **has never been** to India. She would like to go there one day.

5 Jim **has been** to Japan twice. He loved it.

6 I **have not tried** windsurfing, but I'd like to!

7 Jack **has gone** to a movie, I'm not sure when he'll be back.

47

47.1 ◀))

1 I **have been** to five countries on vacation this year.

2 Sandra **has passed** all her medical exams so far this year. I'm so proud.

3 I **visited** Warsaw in 2007 with my family.

4 I'm feeling sleepy. I **haven't had** any coffee yet this morning.

5 My boyfriend **phoned** me last night.

6 Paula's feeling sad. Her dog **died** last week.

7 I'm going to Berlin tomorrow. I **have been** there three times before.

8 I don't have any money. I **lost** my wallet yesterday.

9 This is such a good festival. I **have made** lots of new friends.

10 My sister is really happy. She **passed** her driving test yesterday.

11 I **have played** tennis six times this week. And I'm playing again tomorrow.

47.2

1 Rick has won five gold medals.

2 Rick injured his knee.

3 The next world athletics event is in December.

4 Rick first became famous five years ago.

5 He has done lots of gardening and has spent time with his family.

47.3 ◀))

1 We have never eaten Chinese food.

2 Sharon has seen that movie before.

3 I have played cricket three times in my life.

4 Natasha has visited Rio de Janeiro three times.

5 Yuri hasn't phoned his grandmother.

6 Eddy has bought a new car for his son.

7 Karen has forgotten her ticket for the concert.

47.4 ◀))

1 Can you tell Samantha about the party? **I've already told her.**

2 Has Rico taken his exam? **No, he hasn't taken it yet.**

3 Am I too late for the game? **No, the game hasn't started yet.**

4 What time is Dewain arriving? **He's already arrived.**

5 I'll order the taxi now. **I've already ordered it!**

6 Has the plane from Lisbon landed? **It's already landed.**

7 Has Claire finished her exercises? **No, she hasn't done them yet.**

8 Have you done your project? **Sorry, I haven't started it yet.**

9 Have Bob and Jane gone back home? **Yes, they've already left.**

47.5

1 True **2** False **3** False **4** True

5 True **6** False **7** False

47.6 ◀))

1 I've **already** read that book.

2 I haven't seen the new movie **yet**.

3 Chrissie has **already** left for work.

4 The soccer game hasn't started **yet**.

5 I haven't passed my test **yet**.

6 I've **already** visited that castle twice.

7 Has the party started **yet**?

8 I've **already** ordered the taxi.

9 Malik has **already** emailed Dan.

10 Has Terry cleaned his room **yet**?

11 Tony's **already** made the sandwiches.

12 I've **already** ordered pizza for everyone.

13 Julia hasn't cooked the dinner **yet**.

14 She hasn't been to London **yet**.

15 Ali has **already** bought some milk.

16 Has Tim phoned his grandmother **yet**?

17 Sanjay hasn't sold his car **yet**.

47.7 ◀))

1 She hasn't walked the dog yet.

2 She's hasn't sent the emails yet.

3 She's already bought the fruit and vegetables.

4 She has already bought a present for Claire.

5 She hasn't phoned the bank yet.

48

48.1 ◀))

1 I'd like the apple pie and ice cream, please.

2 My son would like the tomato soup.

3 I'll have the burger and fries, please.

4 My daughter would like the carrot cake with yogurt.

5 For dessert, I'll have the baked banana with cream.

6 To drink, I'd like mineral water, please.

7 For my appetizer, I'd like the garlic bread.

48.2

1 True **2** False **3** True **4** False

5 True **6** True **7** True **8** False

9 True

48.3

1 The antipasti

2 New potatoes

3 The spaghetti

4 $4.95

48.4 ◀))

1. To start, I'll have the tomato soup.

2. To start, I'd like the tomato soup.

3. To start, can I have the tomato soup.

4. For my main course, I'll have the roast chicken.

5. For my main course, I'd like the roast chicken.

6. For my main course, can I have the roast chicken.

7. For my dessert, I'll have the lemon cheesecake.

8. For my dessert, I'd like the lemon cheesecake.

9. For my dessert, can I have the lemon cheesecake.

49

49.1 ◀))

1 Have you ever played soccer? **Yes, but I prefer rugby.**

2 Have you ever worked abroad? **Yes, I was an English teacher in China.**

3 Have you ever won the lottery? **Yes, I once won $10.**

④ Have you ever seen a ghost? **Yes. I was really scared!**

⑤ Have you ever been to Italy? **Yes, I was in Rome last year.**

⑥ Have you ever played the piano? **Yes, I played the piano at school.**

⑦ Have you ever fallen off your bike? **Yes, I broke my arm.**

⑧ Have you ever been on TV? **Yes, I was on a news program.**

⑨ Have you ever seen a lion? **Yes, when I was at the zoo.**

⑩ Have you ever visited New York? **No, but I'd like to see the Statue of Liberty.**

⑪ Have you ever had a pet? **Yes, I had a cat when I was young.**

⑫ Have you ever been sky diving? **No, I'm scared of heights.**

⑬ Have you ever seen *Shrek*? **Yes, it's a really funny movie.**

⑭ Have you ever been to Paris? **Yes, I saw the Eiffel Tower.**

⑮ Have you ever tried Indian food? **Yes, I love curry.**

49.2

① Hasn't done
② Has done
③ Hasn't done
④ Has done
⑤ Hasn't done

49.3 ◀))

① My **flight** leaves at 5am from London.
② I want to **dive** for treasure in the Pacific Ocean.

③ He learned to **surf** in California.
④ My **luggage** got lost when I changed flights.
⑤ I checked into the **hotel** at 10pm.

49.4 ◀))

① We **have never seen** a Shakespeare play, but we **really want** to see one.

② Steve **has never played** a musical instrument, but he **really wants** to learn one.

③ I have **never written** a novel, but I **really want** to do so one day.

④ Esteban has **never eaten** Chinese food, but he **really wants** to try some.

⑤ Ethan has **never seen** a wolf, but he **really wants** to photograph one.

⑥ Stef has **never played** golf, but she **really wants** to try it one day.

⑦ Tommy has **never been** to America, but he **really wants** to go there.

⑧ They have **never stayed** in a hotel, but they **really want** to.

⑨ Doug has **never ridden** a horse, but he **really wants** to try it.

⑩ Marge has **never won** the lottery, but she **really wants** to someday.

⑪ Kimberley has **never flown** in an airplane, but she **really wants** to do it.

⑫ Landon has **never climbed** a mountain, but he **really wants** to visit the Rockies.

⑬ Our children have **never been** to a movie theater, but they **really want** to go.

⑭ We have **never traveled** around South America, but we **really want** to.

⑮ Olivia has **never eaten** olives, but she **really wants** to try them.

⑯ I have **never seen** an action movie, but I **really want** to see one.

⑰ Emily has **never swum** in the ocean, but she **really wants** to try it.

⑱ Melvin has **never done** a parachute jump, but he **really wants** to do one.

⑲ Pete has **never seen** a tiger, but he **really wants** to travel to India.

⑳ Patti has **never been** to the theater, but she **really wants** to go.

㉑ Mary has **never left** her country, but she **really wants** to travel abroad.

49.5 ◀))

① I've never swum in the ocean, but my wife and I are going to Tahiti for our anniversary.

② My boyfriend's never been to Paris, but I'm taking him there for his birthday.

③ My daughter's never seen a tiger, but we're taking her to the zoo on the weekend.

④ I've never tried Chinese food, but my colleagues are taking me to a restaurant in Chinatown next week.

49.6 ◀))

1. I really want to visit Europe.
2. I really want to visit the Taj Mahal.
3. I really want to travel around Europe.
4. I really want to eat some chocolate.
5. I'd like to visit Europe.
6. I'd like to visit the Taj Mahal.
7. I'd like to travel around Europe.
8. I'd like to eat some chocolate.

Acknowledgments

The publisher would like to thank:

Jo Kent, Trish Burrow, and Emma Watkins for additional text; Thomas Booth, Helen Fanthorpe, Helen Leech, Carrie Lewis, and Vicky Richards for editorial assistance; Stephen Bere, Sarah Hilder, Amy Child, Fiona Macdonald, and Simon Murrell for additional design work; Simon Mumford for maps and national flags; Peter Chrisp for fact checking, Penny Hands, Amanda Learmonth, and Carrie Lewis for proofreading; Elizabeth Wise for indexing; Tatiana Boyko, Rory Farrell, Clare Joyce, and Viola Wang for illustrations; Liz Hammond for editing audio scripts and managing audio recordings; Hannah Bowen and Scarlett O'Hara for compiling audio scripts; IDAudio for mixing and mastering audio recordings; Heather Hughes, Tommy Callan, Tom Morse, Gillian Reid, and Sonia Charbonnier for creative technical support; Priyanka Kharbanda, Suefa Lee, Shramana Purkayastha, Isha Sharma, Sheryl Sadana for editorial support; Yashashvi Choudhary, Jaileen Kaur, Bhavika Mathur, Richa Verma, Anita Yadav, Apurva Agarwal for design support; Deepak Negi and Nishwan Rasool for picture research; Rohan Sinha for managerial and moral support.

DK would like to thank the following for their kind permission to reproduce photographs:
67 **Dreamstime.com:** Tamas Bedecs / Bedecs (top right). 87 ImageState / **Alamy:** Pictor (center top), 147 **Getty Images:** James Oliver / Digital Vision (top right)

All other images are copyright DK. For more information, please visit **www.dkimages.com.**